SMALL GARDENS
with Style

SMALL GARDENS
with Style

JILL BILLINGTON

Photographs by
CLIVE NICHOLS

LONDON   NEW YORK   SYDNEY   TORONTO

To Bill, Freya and Griselda

A WARD LOCK BOOK

First published in the UK in 1994
by Ward Lock Ltd
Villiers House, 41/47 Strand
London WC2N 5JE

A Cassell Imprint

This edition published in 1994
by BCA by arrangement with Cassell plc

Distributed in the United States
by Sterling Publishing Co. Inc.
387 Park Avenue South, New York, NY 10016-8810

Distributed in Australia
by Capricorn Link (Australia) Pty Ltd
2/13 Carrington Road, Castle Hill, NSW 2154

A British Library Cataloguing in Publication Data block for this book
may be obtained from the British Library

CN 4090

Garden plans by Jill Billington
Illustrations by Jonathan Adams

Page make-up and typesetting by Associated Print Production Ltd, London
Printed and bound in Spain by Cronion S.A., Barcelona

Frontispiece: Clipped box emphasizes structure in this richly
foliaged town garden.

Contents

Introduction

So much love, so much labour, so much money in so many cultures and for so many centuries – all devoted to this essentially ephemeral art form. How we *care*. Gardens have been a part of life probably since prehistoric times, and now that time appears to be accelerating the need to surround ourselves with natural elements, albeit in a small and personal landscape, has intensified. Co-existing with this is a desire to reaffirm our individuality in this mass-producing world: to flex our creative muscles and make something singular. So our precious space becomes a place for green and spiritual refreshment.

THE SMALL GARDEN

Small gardens have their own problems and virtues. They are often inward looking and intimate. They exclude the world and are intrinsically attractive and reassuringly private. There are fewer incidentals to confuse the design; that is, there are unlikely to be major topographical problems or other complications. However, scale can be a problem. It is always important to provide room for people to move or sit comfortably, so paths should usually be at least 1m (3ft) wide and sitting space convenient. It is also necessary to recognize that both practical requirements and prevailing conditions will affect choices and influence design possibilities. In a small space, you cannot have it all. Just as this is acknowledged in the home, selection must be practised in the outdoor space as well. There is a temptation to 'over design' and the hardest part is to recognize this, have courage and eliminate some of your ideas, however individually attractive they may be. It is only too easy to be seduced by detail and be reluctant to dispose of it, but in the end it is better to do so – after all, what woman wears all her jewellery at once? Selection is an artistic decision, and all the arts are the poorer when the creator has been unable to resist gilding his or her lily. Not only is small beautiful, but so is simple.

Many of us have only very small plots in which we can indulge ourselves, so choices have to be restricted. To some, a small garden is just somewhere to put out the pram or dry the washing – both most justifiable uses of precious and private outdoor space – yet rarely is the small yard completely concreted over. Even those who insist that they don't know the difference between a dandelion and a foxglove often keep an area of grass, and grow a lilac and an apple tree. Concrete would have been simpler: the instinct for greenery will out. Others, of course, go to the opposite extreme of lavishing more time and money on their garden

Opposite: A Garden Divided (see page 30). From the garden room the view is intimately inviting.

than they do on their house, leading one to speculate as to which is actually seen as 'home'.

INSPIRATION – AND PRACTICALITIES

The aim of this book is to show how very different our personal ambitions for the small garden can be. Despite the limited size, there is a wide variety of options open to the owner and I have tried to demonstrate some of these. The imagination is limitless so a book cannot be totally comprehensive, and I have therefore made personal choices, covering familiar types and styles as well as new ideas and developments.

Firstly, I should say that to me, garden design is an art form. It may be unconsciously or consciously enjoyed as such, but it is not simply about horticulture. Nor is it about rectangles of grass surrounded by borders. Most gardeners want more than this, but many are unclear about their own intentions. I hope that by selecting gardens with quite different aims, the book will help readers to consolidate their own ideas.

Can garden design be only about what you want? Well, regrettably not. It would be difficult to grow Mediterranean plants in cooler latitudes or plant a swamp cypress in a container on a roof garden. Of course we accept this, but I should emphasize here that practicalities are fundamental and some chapters in the book refer to this; Chapter 4, for example, deals with 'user-friendly' gardens, Chapter 7 with the requirements for front gardens which have to share space with dustbins and the car. Real constraints do exist and cannot be ignored.

This is a tall order. The gardener has to be aware of the many influential factors which will affect the ultimate look of his or her garden. The land may be very flat; the aspect may well be dominated by neighbouring buildings; the soil could be starved; there will be underground drains and cables. Much has to be considered, and through its various chapters the book will discuss the problems peculiar to a range of different sites and illustrate some of the artful adaptations which are possible.

For horticultural depth, however, you will need to consult expertise elsewhere, and I have provided a bibliography of books which will be helpful in this respect. I have also chosen not to categorize gardens as, for example, water gardens, shade gardens, town courtyards, basement backyards and so forth, as there are already many useful books which classify gardens in this way. Instead, I hope that this book will be inspirational. It is the aesthetic ideals of designing a small garden which are my concern and I have aimed to show how people can achieve this in highly individual ways. After all, when you get down to it the main concern of a gardener is, essentially, how the garden will *look*.

THE FEATURED GARDENS – CASE STUDIES

Each chapter discusses the creative intention of the designers featured and shows how, by using the right design principles, individual garden styles can be realized effectively.

Often, small gardens are in cities and this can be extremely influential, particularly when the main desire of the owner is to deny the locale and select plants which evoke the countryside or wilderness – true *'Rus in urbe'*. Alternatively, these gardeners may plant shrubs with such overlapping density that the city surround is banned from view. These aspects are discussed in Chapter 1. Sometimes, more prosaic demands like family use or entertaining are basic programmes but the gardens chosen are still expected to be beautiful, so these are included in Chapter 2.

Gardens can be spiritually refreshing, and often are. In some cases this can be achieved by romantic, overflowing and bountiful planting, with rustic details, fragrances and fountains. The 'secret gardens' of childhood memories which soothe away troubles, and gardens of fantasy 'with walls and towers girdled round', are gardens of the imagination. Curtains of ivy can be lifted to reveal hidden wonders – gardens of the senses, planned with mystical associations. Romance can also be found when gardens remind us of times past, of other ages when 'parterres' (see Chapter 5) and roses mingled with arbours, or of far-off places where the whole flavour of a garden style can be quite different. Romance in a garden has very strong appeal and is covered in Chapter 3.

Chapter 4, as mentioned earlier, shows how the practical requirements of easy maintenance can be combined with effective design and planting in a variety of ways, to create gardens which look good all year round with the minimum of care. Food growing is also a practical requirement for some, of course, so Chapter 5 explains how to combine the fruit and vegetables with decorative planting and still feed the family – though no low maintenance here!

The next chapter is devoted to the true plant lover. For very many people this is the most compulsive reason for creating a garden, but to make it beautiful, as well as botanically fascinating, requires considerable artistic flair. In Chapter 6 you will see how very differently some creative people have explored this passion.

A 'tidy garden', so often the garden-centre approach, need not be visually poor. If tidiness is really the aim this is easily achieved: slab the whole thing over, go indoors and forget it. Really? So tidiness is not actually the right word. I am reminded of the confusion at the hairdresser when the poor stylist is asked to create a 'tidy style'. Why bother to go in? Why not have it all shaved? That is tidy. No, though customers do mean 'neat' and 'easy to manage', primarily they want it to be flattering. So too with the small garden, and especially the front garden. Often this 'tidy' requirement can be translated as 'easy to care for', 'space for the car', and 'permanently attractive whatever the season'. All this can be achieved with style, as Chapter 7 shows.

The last two chapters deal with less familiar ground. So often the small garden is treated rather conventionally and, as this is a book about inspiration, it seems to me that contemporary designs must be considered, just as 'new' architecture gradually impinges on everyday life. Reproduction 'Regency' furniture or neo-colonial house styles have their

This design by Dan Pearson shows a wonderful use of colour.

place and are reassuring in their familiarity, but new images can be very beautiful too and some of the gardens included here are evidence of this.

I could not let the opportunity go for including some originals. Many people have gardens which are uniquely personal, like one I have seen where the owner made his own concrete slabs and pressed family mementoes into them as they set: coins, pieces of china, a tiny child's car, a set of buttons, little hand and paw prints, and so on. It is, indeed, uniquely personal, amusing and charmingly carried out. In another garden I saw concrete casts made from egg boxes, which provided textured surfaces for rectangular plant containers and plinths on which *objets trouvés* were placed. A New Jersey gardener made casts of his footprints, which became stepping stones – fortunately, he had large feet. And if this were not sufficient, weatherproof woolly 'sheep', concrete 'cows', and of course gnomes of both good and ill-humoured character, have all been seen in gardens. And why not? However, the last gardens in this book are not so much novelty gardens as real explorations of style, providing visions of originality which may well prove influential.

Throughout, the chapters show wide creative differences and interpretations of a site. In many cases, it will be found that the restrictions imposed by the site can actually help with the design process: that problems generate solutions is a truism. So look on problems as friendly indicators – they are often far easier to deal with than the inhibiting, totally empty space of virgin territory. Within the chapters some gardens are studied in great detail, showing how they were planned and the way in which the initial idea progressed into the finished image. Drawings and photographs clarify the method and suggest ideas which are in line with the style principles. For additional interest, gardens are included where the aim is the same, but the interpretation totally different.

You will like some gardens more than others. This in itself can be very helpful, as it is often only by rejecting some ideas that you come to recognize what you really want. I would suggest that clarity of vision is the key: deciding what character of garden most appeals to you, as well as fulfils your requirements, is the first stage of the design process. Once identified, staying with this so that there is a 'wholeness' to the design will produce the greatest reward. There are many ideas to choose from and detailed images often overlap, but initial clear thinking will help a great deal when creating your own utopia.

Some of the gardens were expensive to make while others were not. Some were designed professionally and others, with equal flair, by non-professionals and you will have your own ideas on this. In some cases expensive contractors carried out the work and in others the owners themselves set to, laid every slab and planted every plant. The options are here to see, and I hope that there are styles and ideas in this book which will appeal to every gardener and indeed prove inspirational.

1·Rural Islands in the City

'...to create an illusion of one's own tranquil green space in which no one can trespass and where surrounding buildings can be ignored.'

Probably the first priority of the city gardener is an enfolding greenness. Many gardens in cities or suburbs are small plots, allocated randomly by builders and planners to apartments or houses in densely built-up areas, with unattractive surroundings and often poor soil. However small the plot may be, it is there, and the owner has the opportunity to use it for the simple pleasure of growing plants, as well as the more complicated territorial pleasure of making his or her own mark. In either case, the need to shut out the surroundings becomes a priority; to create an illusion of one's own tranquil green space in which no one can trespass and where surrounding buildings can be ignored.

There are different ways of tackling this. Concealing surroundings can be achieved physically, by screening with either fencing, walling or plants, or alternatively by psychological methods, where the attention is distracted from the displeasing to the alluring. In many cases a combination of both will achieve the aim.

To create your city 'island', you do need to take a good look at the surroundings to assess what should be concealed. It may not always be possible to achieve this completely; a tower block, for example, is not the easiest thing to hide. However, if you create a beautiful and arresting garden it will captivate attention, and the surroundings then cease to be relevant. Yet it is still more reassuring to mask an unpleasing locale completely if at all possible, and the first garden described here is a very good example of this.

CASE STUDY

Greened Peace

This house and garden are in an urban residential area. Initially the land at the back was undeveloped. However, a new estate of closely packed town houses was planned which would affect the view enormously and also reduce any prospect of privacy, as the houses were to be only a few paces from the back fence.

The photographs on pages 13 and 16 show the garden as it was before work was started. One, taken from the house, shows the rectangular shape clearly, emphasized by the line of snow along the fence. When the housing development materialized, though not unattractive, it completely dominated the view. The second photograph shows the uncompromising and bare rectangularity of the plot. All the neighbouring properties on either side of this house had exactly the same size and shape of garden, which ran in parallel towards the proposed development. It was a real challenge to see what could be done to make this space both private and personal, as well as screening it from all the surroundings.

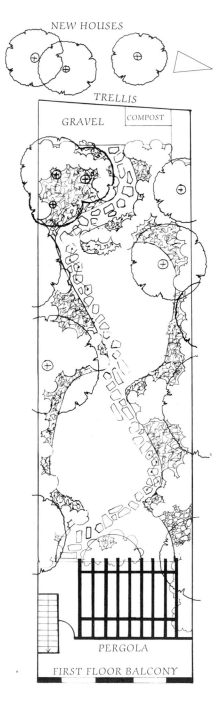

NEW HOUSES

TRELLIS

GRAVEL COMPOST

PERGOLA

FIRST FLOOR BALCONY

Greened Peace
This plan shows how a rigidly rectangular
site can be concealed by a layout of fluid
abstract shapes.

FIRST STEPS – BORROWING FROM THE LANDSCAPE After
surveying the nearly empty site and thinking about what, if anything,
could be saved for use in the new garden, the owners and I realized that
only the mature neighbouring trees which overhang the side boundaries
could serve the scheme well. These would be influential in as much as
they dictated where new trees could *not* go. But they were also an asset,
as they could be incorporated within the new plan. Often a design can
benefit from surrounding planting by linking the plants within the
garden to those outside, obscuring the actual line of demarcation that is
the real boundary.

The notion of 'borrowing' landscape is not new. Japanese garden
designers were great practitioners of this skill, which is known as
shakkei. Originally, country views of mountains and hills served as a
backdrop for great country gardens like those around Kyoto, but as the
space allocated to houses decreased, just as it did in the west, this art was
refined by careful planting which shut out the city and focused upon
intimate views of distant hills wherever possible. In this garden there
were no distant views, but the neighbouring trees could be 'borrowed' on
the *shakkei* principle and provide an apparent continuity of planting
pattern.

This idea was taken further. At the far end, where the new houses were
to be built, there was plenty of room for new trees beyond the boundary
of the garden. The owners approached the developers and gained their
permission to pay for and plant some silver birch (*Betula pendula*) within
the new development and behind their own fence. This fitted in well
with the landscaping of the estate, so the developers were pleased to
agree.

The garden owners then planted a group of white-barked *Betula utilis*
var. *jacquemontii* within their own boundary, and the two groups created
an instant visual link.

The birches are deliberately not identical, as the new garden was to be
planted in a very considered way. The silver birches outside, now
thriving amongst the new houses, are the wild European silver birch
which is tough and reliable and needs no special care. *Betula utilis* var.
jacquemontii, on the other hand, is not indigenous and comes from the
Himalayas. It is a less pendulous tree, being rather stiff in habit, but it has
a most dazzlingly white bark. A group of three were planted at the far
end of the garden about 2.4m (8ft) from the boundary, where they look
as beautiful in winter as in summer.

THE LAYOUT The plan was then drawn up with simple abstract shapes.
Certain requirements were very important. The owners were determined
to lose the geometry of the rectangle. They also wanted to create a
framework which would to conceal the boundaries all year round, so the
external, bounded shape of the space was to be ill defined and of little
consequence. Instead, the green rhythms of the interior were to create
tranquillity, a virtue which underlies many of the world's great gardens.

Above: Before – From the balcony the uncompromising long, thin rectangular site can be seen, with snow marking the north-facing boundary. The underdeveloped land at the far end awaits the housing estate, now completed, which would have completely dominated the view.

Right: After – The mature, redesigned garden, viewed from the balcony, encloses intimate spaces and excludes everything beyond its boundaries.

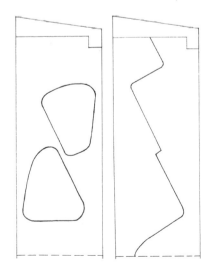

Fig 1 (left) 'Organic' triangles.

Fig 2 (right) A diagonal path cuts across the rectangle.

The plan opposite shows the actual layout which provides the 'bones' of the design. Ideas of dividing the space into two quite separate units were considered but then rejected, as the house is part of a tall, unbroken terrace of similar properties and greater unity and harmony could be achieved by making a very simple shape flowing from it without interruption. Nonetheless, there are actually four linked areas in the garden. An area for sitting in peaceful contemplation looks out from beneath the vine canopy of the pergola on to what are virtually two triangular, but 'organically' shaped, spaces, bonded together as one. They almost divide the garden on the diagonal. A simplified line drawing (Fig 1) illustrates this. Through such means the sense of space is unspecified, and by implication greatly increased. This device also helped to create a path, cutting diagonally across the rectangle, negotiating the gap sideways and continuing along a parallel diagonal to curve round at the far end, where it serves the hidden utility area. Fig 2 shows how the path cuts directly across the rectangle, but is neither obviously diagonal nor disruptively straight. The enclosing forms are far more significant.

The photograph above shows the new garden layout clearly. The eye is drawn to the distance, though the end of the garden is unclear. There is at all times an awareness of breadth, as the abstract shapes of the grass make maximum use of the real width of the garden. In places the edges of the lawn come to within 30cm (1ft) of the fence. Where this occurs, massed evergreens such as the bamboo *Sasa veitchii* and scrambling ivies conceal the fence. (As this bamboo is invasive it must be contained below ground by a slate 'wall' or some similar hard barrier.) So green grass meets greened fence, and the boundary melts away.

At the far end a 2m (6ft) wide service area is gravelled and allows plenty of space for composts. This is completely invisible from the house, being screened by *Viburnum tinus*, *Eleagnus ebbingei* and a clump of the relatively uninvasive bamboo *Arundinaria murieliae*. Two metres beyond this, ivy- and rose-clad trellis 2.4m (8ft) high adds to the privacy. This hidden service area is reached by the stepping-stone path as it curves around out of sight from the house, thus increasing the suggestion of further unspecified space beyond.

As described earlier, the path actually bisects the garden on the diagonal. It is laid very carefully and 'sidesteps' to the right where the narrow neck occurs, between the two garden areas. Here I must mention that the garden owners had lived in Japan for some years. They had no intention of trying to create a Japanese garden, but were very keen to remind themselves of the beauty and spirit of the great gardens of that country. Detailing the path was extremely important and was carried out over a period of days, with discussion and reference to photographs brought back from Japan. A stepping-stone path was chosen because it would not be too dominant. It was important to avoid laying the stones in a straight line; in Japan the pattern can relate to the flight path of birds, which can be slow and elegant or quick and darting, but here the aspirations were more modest – yet a gently expressed zig-zag, dictated by easy walking, did fit the requirements well. The stones chosen were of different sizes and shapes, some dressed and some not. Two long, straight stones preceded by a square set at 45° worked very well, as they move the action sideways when encountering the further grassed space.

The owners also derived much pleasure from siting a Yukimigata lantern below the plum tree. This was done with a certain amount of humour, as they are very well aware that this is not a Japanese garden, but they found it irresistible. Equally agreeable is the careful training of a blue conifer, as learned when in Tokyo; a blue picea is being gently trained on a bamboo frame with carefully tied knots, as can be seen in the photograph.

THE PLANTING Some Japanese influences are again evident in the planting. The great white cherry (*Prunus* 'Tai Haku') balances the plum. As mentioned, bamboo has been used in several areas, paeonies provide both flower and foliage, wisteria climbs the balustrade and house walls, small pines create structural form. The sacred bamboo (*Nandina domestica*) has a place and, of course, there are acers. Linear patterns are taken up with irises, sisyrinchium, grasses, day lilies and liatris. Beneath the *Betula utilis* var. *jacquemontii* are hostas, ferns, *Euphorbia robbiae* and

A blue picea is being carefully trained on a bamboo frame.

Phormium cookianum variegatum provides a dramatic focus in front of the vine-clad pergola. Another container holds a magnificent *Pinus strobus.*

Lamium maculatum 'White Nancy'. Foliage and form dominate. The shrubs around the boundaries create green walls, and against these dwarf pines, clipped box, a white shrubby potentilla, some pale roses, small fuschias and, at lower level, spreading junipers maintain a very lush, largely evergreen environment.

Like the simplicity of the layout, the plants have been chosen to blend in with one another. There is a very limited colour range. In fact, it is very nearly a totally, but not a uniformly, green garden. Some pastel flowers and a few bluish or variegated leaves add subtle colour, but the restricted colour range adds greatly to the tranquillity and peace of the whole.

The owners have visual flair and add annuals in pots, moving them around as the herbaceous plants go past their best. Usually these are white marguerites, which light up corners and announce 'summer' in this all-year-round garden. Other containers hold some unusual choices: the phormium in the photograph above is particularly striking.

15

Left: Before – Looking back at the house the view is austere. Compare this with the photograph below, where the pergola carries the green of the wall climbers down to garden level.

Below: After – The view from beneath the plum tree to the back of the house shows the transformation of the garden.

Sitting within the pergola, listening to the gentle sound of the wind chimes and looking out to the lush green garden, it is hard to believe that this is actually an urban environment.

Regarding the garden as a whole, the owners value the changes of the seasons, from the greening in spring to the flare of autumn, and when winter frost covers the grass the dark pattern of the stepping stones takes over a dominant role and becomes the dramatic focus. At all times, these garden lovers have continued to care for their green space with discriminating affection. What is beyond the perimeters is now irrelevant – the photographs show that this is truly an island of its own with very personal touches. The photograph opposite shows the view looking back towards the house, and it is interesting to compare this with the 'before' photograph. The 'neck' of the garden, where the stepping stones move sideways, is marked by matching *Viburnum davidii* specimens. Foliage can be seen climbing up the steps, wisteria on one side and *Parthenocissus tricuspidata* on the other, blending house with garden. The pergola is visible, extending the geometry of the house out over the paving to the garden. It supports a magnificent *Vitis vinifera* 'Purpurea', thus also linking the foliage down to ground level. The photograph on page 17 shows the view from under this canopy, framed by the simple but strong timber structure of posts, rafters and beams, and the mellow sound of wind chimes adds to the rustle of the leaves. This secluded, loggia-like pergola provides dappled shade in the hottest part of the garden and from it the view is green, enclosed and private. Compare this with that of a few years ago, on page 13.

CASE STUDY

Pooled Planting

Whereas the first garden is rather deceptive, in that it is far more deliberately planned than it would appear and the plants are all carefully selected garden varieties, the second garden creates the illusion of being far removed from city life, as within it lies a pool with surrounding plants which could have been entirely natural.

The townscape is irrelevant in this delightful 'wilderness within a garden', shown in the photograph opposite. The owner is a knowledgeable plantswoman who, as well as living a full professional life, also maintains a large allotment and runs a family home. Plants, carefully selected to take care of themselves, fill the space with well-judged abandon. The wildlife pool attracts frogs, toads, water snails and newts as companions for green tench. Hedgehogs and cats run free. The whole atmosphere is one of a semi-woodland natural pond which is unkempt but charming and gives little indication of the city surround.

In fact, the pond was made in what was originally a rather formal, small brick-walled garden. Mature fruit trees and a large pampas grass were all that existed, making an ordinary and unexciting plot. Instead of working out a design, the owner decided that a semi-wild pond would be far more attractive and interesting. There is no path or patio, just collections of shade plants under the trees and some unusual climbers allowed the freedom to compete over walls and up trees. The rest is grass.

THE POND With positive ideas of what was wanted from both the pond and associated bog garden, the owner did the work herself. A hole was dug nearly 60cm (2ft) deep and roughly 2.1m (7ft) long by 1m (3ft) across. Allowance was made for the bog garden, which was to be as important as the pool. The shape appears to be random, but is basically an oval which is wider at one end than the other – simple shapes are always best. As a general rule, the bigger the pool the more likelihood there is of achieving an ecological balance and stable water temperature, although obviously in a small garden the size has to be restricted. As regards the position of the pool, even if the garden is small you should aim at a site which is not too shaded, with approximately four to five hours of sunlight on the water. Avoid trees immediately overhead, as falling leaves decompose in the water and no one wants a bubbling soup.

In this case, the water is not agitated in any way. There is no pump, but in case of flooding a run-off has been provided. A butyl liner extends beyond the pool edge, underlying the bog garden. Most of the edges are smoothly sloped, but the side facing the camera is a particularly gentle slope. The 'shallows' provide for marginal plants which need their feet in water but do not wish to drown. The owner did not want to add even a randomly paved edging, so the grass just merges into the bog, with the occasional group of pebbles. In fact, this is quite a difficult act to pull off – such an innocently natural look can only be maintained with some care and understanding. If you do undertake to make a pool yourself it is a good idea to read a useful book on the subject first, and the bibliography includes some suggestions.

THE PLANTING As regards the planting, there are very many options, but in this case the owner had a particular interest in indigenous plants, adding only a few garden varieties to create an interesting collection. *Rheum palmatum* 'Atrosanguineum' and the flag iris (*Iris pseudacorus*) provide the structural planting, with an orange-flowered

Almost a naturalist's garden, the pool and marsh planting shown here were created on site and not planned on paper.

mimulus, blue water forget-me-not (*Myosotis palustris*), water speedwell (*Veronica anagallis aquatica*) and North American pickerel weed (*Pontederia cordata*) adding colour. Meadowsweet (*Filipendula ulmaria* syn. *Spiraea ulmaria*), deliberately planted, fosters the wild theme as do the bog bean (*Menyanthes trifoliata*), common lady's smock (*Cardamine pratense*) and sweet flag (*Acoruscalamus*). Interweaving along the edges, mixing with grass, are bog arum (*Calla palustris*) and tufted sedge (*Carex acuta*). In the water, pygmy water lilies and arrowhead (*Sagittaria sagittifolia*) fight it out, though nature is certainly assisted by the knowledge of the owner.

This is an unusual pond, requiring a real interest in plants from both wild and garden sources. If you intend to make your own pond you do need to decide whether it is to be formal or informal, have flowing, moving water or a still, reflecting surface, and whether to include a bog. Wildlife ponds can be very attractive, encouraging frogs, water snails and dragonflies, as well as supporting fish and newts. But, like wildlife gardens, they are actually much harder to create and maintain than the formal garden pool and do require that you are prepared to read a little, observe and learn from mistakes.

It is worth noting here that not all gardens need to be drawn up on paper to be attractive and successful. Certainly, working on paper can help to clarify intentions and avoid expensive mistakes, but not everyone works well in two dimensions and this should never prevent anyone from enjoying making a garden.

GARDENING WITH NATURE

Creating a wild garden within a small urban plot would be a way of denying the presence of the town, and making a garden that appears to regenerate itself with minimal interference does sound appealing. Many are tempted and wild flowers are in vogue, but I have misgivings. Sweeps of meadows, cropped by cows, producing a mixture of delicately simple flowers with additions of more colourful poppies and cornflowers are part of the green movement. They have an air of charming naturalness which evokes a childhood that most of us in the late twentieth century never had. I suspect that nostalgia is as much a part of this as is any desire to preserve nature. Wild gardens can be very beautiful but can also be harder to manage than conventional gardens, and therein lies the problem. What *is* a really wild garden? It should mean brambles, ground ivy and nettles, all of which will provide cover for wildlife. It must relate to the type of soil on which you garden, as truth to nature is an integral part of the concept. In the small garden space this can be acknowledged rather than achieved. The pool garden already described has successfully attracted dragonflies, insects and hedgehogs, despite being in the metropolis, proving that this is possible. Most people know which plants will attract butterflies and will choose plants with this aim in mind. But to create a rural museum within your plot does not necessarily mean that all the selected plants are beautiful – in the garden context, that is.

Part of the problem is that in the wild plants grow in massed drifts, as they have dispersed themselves, but scale is important in the small garden and drifts are not so easy to achieve. The other difficulty is that plants in the wild are very seasonally conscious. They have not been bred for extended flowering periods as have garden plants, so the scene can be disappointing for a large part of the year. Compromise and subtle planning could be the answer. In place of masses you could plant in small meanders, and in place of short seasons considered planning could create overlaps of seasonal flowering, by introducing a denser concentration of plants than one would find in the wild.

DESIGNING A NATURAL GARDEN

If you are particularly keen on a very rural look, I would suggest that you do design your plot, but so subtly that there is no evidence of this. You could create winding shapes, which sweep rather than wriggle, and if the other elements of the garden, apart from the plants, are chosen with care, like wood-chip or gravel paths, steps made from split logs and random-shaped boulders and slabs of local rock as features, the imagery will be complete.

You could provide a shade area for all the wild shade-loving plants like wood anemone, spurge, foxglove, wood violet, martagon lilies, creeping dogwood, bugle, asarum, wood garlic and so forth, with a canopy and backing of shrubs with hips and haws and old man's beard (*Clematis vitalba*). Then perhaps include in the garden a sunny area, for which there are many choices, which could be enclosed with dog rose, guelder rose, elder and small willows.

But there are alternative ideas which could suggest a natural rather than a wild garden – ferns and grasses, for instance, could be very stylish alternatives. Both types of plant allude to the wild, yet both are luxuriously leaved for much of the year.

The patterns of grasses can be gracefully reflexed or proudly upright. They can be as tall as the pampas grass (*Cortaderia selloana*) which can reach 3.6m (12ft), or very short like *Festuca varia* ssp *scoparia*. They may have fluffy panicles which catch the light like tufted hair grass (*Deschampsia caespitosa*), or gleamingly combed panicles like the Chinese silver grass (*Miscanthus sinensis*), which is a great deal taller. Some are very blue like blue lyme grass (*Elymus arenarius*), a coarsely invasive grass if grown in sandy soil, or blue fescue (*Festuca glauca*). Then there are yellow-striped grasses like tiger grass (*Miscanthus sinensis* 'Zebrinus'), which is also tellingly known as porcupine grass, or fully yellow grasses like 'Bowles' Golden Grass (*Milium effusum* 'Aureum'). Also worth considering are Japanese blood grass (*Imperata cylindrica* 'Red Baron') and brown *Carex comans*, a small sedge about 45cm (1½ft) high. These are but a very few descriptions, intended to whet your appetite. The list on this page adds more alternatives.

As you can see in the photograph below, mixing grass-like perennials like *Sisyrinchium striatum*, irises, kniphofia and *Schizostylis coccinea* in amongst the grasses can add a dash of colour. Some tall, slender blue *Campanula persicifolia* or the flat heads of achillea varieties would also mix very well. In the photograph, *Sedum spectabile* 'Autumn Joy' and *Physostegia virginiana* also look extremely effective, adding rich deep reds amongst their reedy companions. In winter some of the grasses are parchment-pale, like *Calamagrostis acutiflora* 'Stricta', or gracefully evergreen, like *Carex albida* which, though only 30cm (1ft) high, is a charming light green.The effect can be very beautiful if the virtues of the sedges, grasses and reeds are fully explored, and the result will be a lush garden style which is not wild but does refer very positively to nature rather than the city environment in which you may grow them.

Ferns also remind one of the countryside without actually being in the image of a wild garden. Like the grasses they have particular requirements as to soils, climate and site, so these are important starting points. They mix well with grasses but would also associate comfortably with acers, particularly green ones, and tall plants like foxgloves, mulleins and lilies. But if the ground is dampish, wonderful foliage contrasts with rodgersia, rheum, ligularia and hostas can be very effective, with a few 'pretties' invited such as dicentra, honesty, astilbe, primulas, irises, cimicifuga *et al*. With all these lush patterns, green hues and gently stirring foliage, the effect will be such that the urban surroundings do not get a look in.

Grass forms flow into one another in this magnificent bed and thoughtfully selected companion planting adds subtle red hues.

2 · Urbane Gardens for Entertaining

'The whole essence of the sophisticated garden is its clarity of style and ease of use.'

Often referred to as 'the room outside', the town yard offers great scope for stylish garden design. The prerequisites are space for entertaining, hard surfaces for easy maintenance and glorious planting which is attractive at every season.

These are gardens which are heavily used. Entertaining alfresco has become a customary adjunct to urban life. Consuming the Sunday papers with relaxed indulgence, unwinding with pre-dinner drinks, viewing a softly lit night landscape from the house are all part of the charms of domesticity in the city. The garden offers many opportunities for pleasurable outdoor living and few spaces are too small to be utilized in this way.

The design should be kept very simple. Features which work well in other styles of garden can easily become irritating and intrusive; too many groups of containers with ever-changing planting, for example, are out of step with the cool refinement of the urbane garden. Restraint is the key. An excess of birdbaths, sundials, urns and statues actually reduces rather than enhances the charm of such gardens. The whole essence of the sophisticated garden is its clarity of style and ease of use. These are not gardens for 'buttons and bows' but more 'couturier' gardens where 'cut' and elegance hold the stage.

Lawn is usually dispensed with. It is inconvenient to place chairs and tables upon it and the space needed to store a mower can be used for better things. These gardens depend upon good-quality paving and beautiful but manageable planting.

CASE STUDY

Through a Glass Lightly

The first garden is a very small courtyard, only 5 x 7m (16 x 23ft), which lies behind early nineteenth-century terraced houses in Hampstead, London. Heavily overshadowed by four-storey houses, it is dark, and was not inviting. The brick-built boundary walls are over 2m (7ft) high, and as the house is on a hill the courtyard is lower than the ground floor, making this quite a sunken garden. Despite the fact that there is only a limited square of sky, the summer sun does reach two of the walls and provides warm light on these for four or five hours.

The previous owners had planted this intimate space with appropriately shade-tolerant, easy-care plants, but a mature *Malus* 'Golden Hornet' has to be thinned regularly. Nevertheless, an established bamboo, *Arundinaria murieliae*, *Mahonia* x *media* 'Charity' and a camellia were ideally sited and provided the foundation planting of the garden.

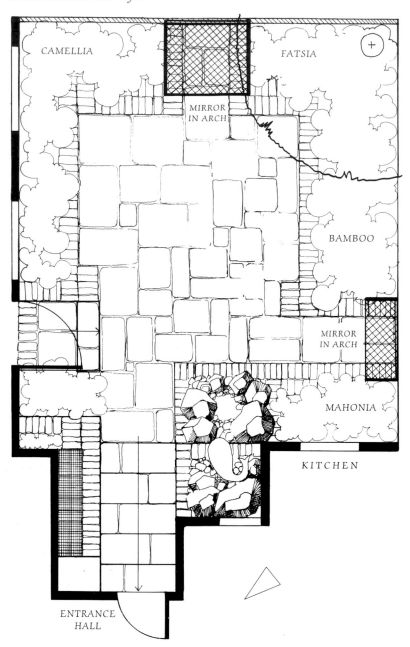

CAMELLIA

FATSIA

MIRROR
IN ARCH

BAMBOO

MIRROR
IN ARCH

MAHONIA

KITCHEN

ENTRANCE
HALL

Through a Glass Lightly
Maximum floor space was crucial to this
plan. Existing plants are identified.

FIRST CONSIDERATIONS The new owners entertain a great deal and
the courtyard is literally an 'outdoor room', which has to work as hard as
any room in the house as well as being attractive at all seasons. The
design therefore provides as much floorspace as possible which is both
uncluttered and on one level. Whenever a table and chairs are used out-
of-doors one must allow 'stretching space' – room for people to push
back their chairs at the coffee stage and extend their possibly six-foot
bodies. If the legs of the chairs slide off the paving and into the soft
planting beds it can be disastrous, so a reliable level space behind each
guest is a priority.

The only detail specifically requested for this backyard was a small water feature to include a bronze-fish fountain. As space was to be so important, this feature was easily tucked into a corner beside the house and steps, providing the gentle sound of water and creating an opportunity to add the attractive shapes of carefully selected, water-worn cobbles.

If you look at the photograph below, which was taken before work started, you can see that there were too many levels. Having come down steep steps from the hall, the visitor had then to step up on to the circle of brick pavers. Added to this, three drains hampered progress as they too were at different levels. In an effort to ease the situation, the hall steps were extended to become more shallow. This helpfully created a small alcove in which the pool and fountain could be sited. The skilled contractor managed to lift and re-bed the manhole covers and drains on to one level, thus reducing the likelihood of accidents.

As a direct result of maximizing the floor area, the planting beds are small. For the same reason, container planting is also restricted in this garden. The only plant containers used are sited to the side of the entrance steps, partially concealing an iron grating but allowing air – and the cat – access to the house via a basement window. One large, important container, planted with the faithful *Aucuba japonica* 'Crotonifolia', is sited level with the top step on a 'shelf' of sandstone.

Below: Before – The original photograph shows a small dark courtyard as it was when the new owners moved in. The levels were over-complicated and the site was dark and moss-covered.

Right: After – Light pierces the dark wall and a mirror-filled arch creates a 'phantom' courtyard beyond.

REFLECTED LIGHT One of the most important considerations was how to increase the light into the garden. In the 'before' photograph on page 25, you can see that this was a very dark site which encouraged a growth of moss on the brick paving, making it slippery and dank. Moss can be charming, as in Japanese gardens, but it can also be hazardous. However, the corner beside the steps faces due south, and to capitalize on direct sunlight it was decided to reflect this into the permanently dark recesses of the opposing walls. Two mirrors were placed on these walls within curved trellised arches. They are as tall as the surrounding walls and both rest on the paving, creating a truly *trompe-l'oeil* effect: the walls are apparently pierced by tunnelled entrances leading to ghost gardens. Using timber arches around the mirrors was important, as they foster the illusion by creating 'paths' which are really niches. Timber diamond-patterned trellis was chosen for the arches. It is painted a soft dove-grey, and links with the wall trellis. No finials distract the eye: it is the 'passage' which is important. The photograph on page 25 taken from the steps shows the view and how effectively a path appears to lead through to the reflected garden beyond. I decided to make the main arch deeper than the side arch, as in this way the eye is drawn to the phantom courtyard in front, while the shallower arch merely indicates an interesting, though illusory, side passage, seen in the photograph opposite.

Sight lines are important. The main mirrored arch is not exactly opposite the steps – the illusion would be completely spoiled if one saw oneself straight away on entering. Rather, as guests come from the hall and down the steps, they see the water feature through arch A (see Fig 1) without immediately realizing that it is actually beside them. The arched passage B becomes evident as one enters the yard, adding to the general feeling of spaciousness in what is really a small and enclosed area. This provides much entertainment and, I am told, makes hostessing initially very easy! Though these features are obviously fun, they also achieve the aim of greatly increasing the light. As the sun touches only two of the walls, and everywhere else is very dark, the reflected light is cheerful, even in winter. Added to this, the once-small courtyard is now comfortably roomy, and this feeling is not confined to the initial impact – even when one is aware that it is 'all done by mirrors', the sense of space persists.

An added bonus for the owners was quite unexpected. As one works by the kitchen windows there is a far greater sense of the garden than previously. In fact, it has proved perfectly possible to maintain conversations with guests sitting on the steps outside whilst stuck at the kitchen sink. Communication is carried on quite normally, by sight as well as verbally, as can be seen in Fig 2, where the lines D–A–C make this possible. I have to admit, though, that this was no ingenuity on the part of the designer.

MATERIALS In a small, sophisticated courtyard such as this, attention to detail is very important. The choice of materials is crucial and can make a great difference to the finished look of the garden. Timber.

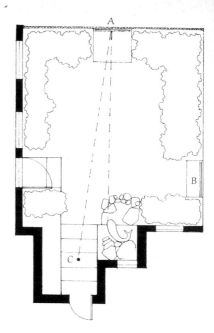

Fig 1 From the hall, apparently looking through arch A to a small pool. In fact the pool is immediately to the right.

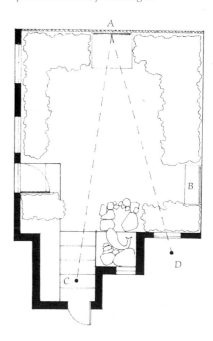

Fig 2 The mirror in arch A acts like a satellite, bouncing communication from the kitchen, D, to the steps, C.

Opposite: A shallower 'archway' to the side leads into another light-filled 'ghost' yard.

Fig 3 Laying flagstones.

Use a smaller flagstone as a 'key' to the design, working around it and expanding outwards from it. Smaller slabs do not look good at the edge of paving and can be a weakness, as any weight placed on them is not widely distributed.

Aim to avoid creating a 'crossroads' where the pointed joints meet, otherwise it will be the jointing, rather than the beauty of the paving, which attracts the eye.

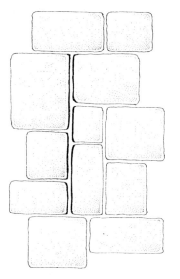

In a similar way, a long straight line of pointing is also too distracting in paving. On the whole, do not allow more than three flagstones to be set in a line before it is interrupted by another stone.

decking was not suitable because in darker, damper areas wood tends to hold moisture. For the same reason, brick paving was not chosen as it attracts moss. The choice was narrowed down to tiles or stone as being the most appropriate materials, and in the end stone was selected, as the house is over 200 years old and it was felt that stone slabs would suit it best. The selected paving is of new sandstone 'flags' which are variously cream and honey coloured. They bring light and warmth into the space and blend well with the existing eighteenth-century brickwork. An edging of old stock bricks is suitably subdued in colour and closely resembles the house bricks.

Laying stone flags in a randomly rectangular pattern should be done with care. There are some principles which, if observed, create a more satisfactory floor plan, and these are shown in the diagrams. This sort of care when carrying out the work is well worth while.

THE PLANTING Despite the lack of planters, there are two areas in this garden which could provide more detailed interest and scope for plants. One is the narrow strip beside the entrance steps as seen in the photograph, which is interesting to compare with the 'before' photograph opposite. Here, culinary herbs in pots and summer-flowering annuals benefit from being in the sun for half the day.

The other feature is the tiny pool, through which water circulates from a bronze fish on to the pebbles below. This can be seen in the photograph opposite. In the raised square bed the fish fountain is in full shade, but as a tiny trickle of water leaks back into the soil from the fish it is always damp. As a result, this is an ideal site for small ferns to grow amongst the pebbles. The soft shield fern (*Polystichum setiferum*) is the largest of these, but the hart's tongue fern (*Asplenium scolopendrium*), American maidenhair (*Adiantum pedatum*) and the tiny spleenwort (*Asplenium trichomanes*) are all flourishing in this slightly acidic soil. The other great success is a *Pittosporum tenuifolium* 'Irene Patterson' from New Zealand, which needs to be grown in a sheltered site. Its mottled, jade undulate foliage is extremely pretty and invaluably evergreen. Though normally a tall shrub, this specimen is constricted by the contained bed but seems to be content, minding neither the complete lack of sun nor having to share the site with the ferns. The soil is deep and is fertilized twice a year.

The rest of the planting in such a small space must be chosen with care and should provide more than one season of interest. On the whole, this is a foliage garden which aims to be attractive at all times. Variegated foliage is an asset as it offers colour. Plants like *Euonymus fortunei* 'Emerald 'n' Gold' or 'Emerald Gaiety' are invaluable as they are evergreen, will do well in shade and are low growing. *Rhamnus alaterna* 'Argenteovariegata' is also useful for the same reasons, except that it is a large shrub and has to be pruned regularly. *Iris foetidissima* 'Variegata' will grow almost anywhere and is attractively bright in darker recesses. However, the flowers are modest and it is sterile, so does not have the

Above: Before – The view looking back to the house.

Right: After – A tiny fountain and pool tuck in neatly beside the shallow steps and the rendered wall is toned down to a soft grey. It is interesting to note the changes compared to the photograph above.

pods of orange fruits which embellish its plain green sibling. Both thrive in this garden. An architectural variegated fatsia also grows very well. Its large palmate leaves add structure which is quite equal to the striking sculpted foliage of the *Mahonia* x *media* 'Charity' sited at the opposite corner.

Climbers are of great importance in such confined spaces. Clematis and roses are colourful and *Parthenocissus henryana*, *Lonicera japonica* 'Aureoreticulata' and assorted ivies add foliage pattern. Shade plants such as *Iris foetidissima* 'Citrina', *Epimedium perralderianum*, *Saxifraga fortunei* 'Wada's Variety', *Viola cornuta* 'Alba' and *Euphorbia robbiae*, all ably assisted by ferns, hostas and astilbes, are the mainstay. Seasonal changes are achieved using bulbs, with *Anemone blanda*, *Nectaroscordium Siculum* and lilies doing well after narcissi have led the way. Two matching clipped *Buxus sempervirens* 'Suffruticosa' on either side of arch A help to restrain the admittedly over-planted lushness. Both arches are wisteria clad, and the foliage and flowers are softening and attractive.

As space for planting is so limited, summer annuals supplement the established plants, adding colour in their season. Of these, there are a few which will adapt to shade. Busy lizzies (*Impatiens*) and selected violas will both grow in shady borders, as will some of the lily family. Dwarf strains of nicotiana can be fitted into the other beds where, as the colour is not too strong, they blend well with the perennials. A clump of *Osteospermum* 'Whirligig' did quite well during one hot summer and some pots of white *Campanula isophylla* were placed amongst the plants in the sunny bed.

Left: Before – The view of the yard from the entrance hall.

Right: After – From the hallway one looks through the arch on to an invitingly sunny courtyard. The sense of space and light is now greatly increased as can be seen by comparing it with the adjacent photograph.

The planting effect can be assisted regularly in this manner, as annuals and half-hardy plants in containers can be moved around to fill gaps in the beds and generally make themselves useful.

In a garden like this great demands are made on the soil. It is always dry and requires regular cossetting and fertilizing, but neither jobs are onerous in such a small space.

So, this once unpromising sunken courtyard has had a complete make-over. As one enters the house and walks along the hall, the new garden can be seen with its sunny courtyard beyond, as the photograph above shows. It is an illusion – but in their own way most gardens are.

CASE STUDY

A Garden Divided

The second garden in this chapter is also one used for entertaining but it is larger, on two levels and far more sunny. The owner is also interested in plants and wanted a richly planted, attractive formal garden. The view from the house windows, the garden room and the balcony are all important.

Although this garden is also within the metropolis it enjoys privacy, as it is not overlooked. The boundary at the far end is a very tall brick wall which is the back of a nineteenth-century mews. Only one small, opaque window breaks the brick pattern and, as long as the light was not blocked, there was little problem in screening this.

The house itself is also an early nineteenth-century building and, like the garden, had been neglected for a long time. The levels of the garden

A Garden Divided
The garden space is on two levels and
serves two functions – it is a luxuriously
planted garden and is spacious enough for
entertaining.

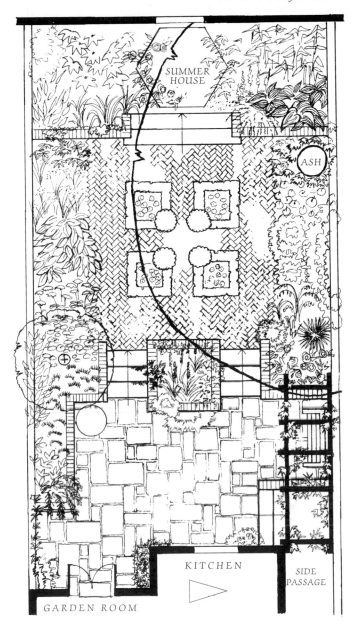

proved to be a slight problem when the builders moved in, making it
necessary to lower the original courtyard so the transition from garden
room to paving was on one level.

A photograph taken of the site before work started shows it unkempt
and unloved (see page 32). At the far end is the mews wall with its small
window, and the confused levels can be seen, with their crumbling, badly
made steps and ragged grass. Two old, but sound, brick walls bound the
garden on either side, and neither neighbour objected to the addition of
trellis to enclose the space and increase seclusion. As with the previous
garden, the urban surroundings offered no views and so this one too was
to be inward looking.

As to planting, only a hydrangea and a viburnum were worth keeping, but there was also a very large sycamore. This affected the garden enormously. However, though one would never plant such a forest-sized tree in a small town garden, permission to remove it was not sought. It does add character with the sheer unpredictability of its presence, and the foliage canopy is charming, as it provides seclusion for the upper floors of the house. The roots must extend a long way but they have not caused problems, whereas removing it might create some.

This tree did, nevertheless, have to be taken into account. Initially the garden was heavily shaded, but the decision was taken to bring in skilled tree surgeons about every three to four years to control the spread of the canopy. This creates some planting problems, as during that time sunny borders gradually become shaded borders which, at the stroke of a chainsaw, quickly become sunny again. The nature of the smaller herbaceous plants has therefore altered over time, but the wall shrubs and climbers seem to have coped well.

THE LAYOUT As regards the layout plan, this is very geometric and virtually symmetrical. Formality suits the house and provides a structured base for horticultural adventures. A wide paved area immediately beside the house is at ground level. Access via the garden room is easy and there is sufficient space for quite a large gathering. A timber arbour covers a seat, providing some shade in the heat of mid-day, and acts also as a vehicle for *Vitis vinifera* 'Brandt', *Parthenocissus quinquefolia* and a scented rose, 'Mme Gregoire Stachelin', to be transported across to the house.

One of the pleasures of gardens is strolling around them and, rather than retracing one's steps, returning by a different route. Often such an aim cannot be achieved in a small garden, but in this case, as can be seen in the photograph opposite, one can truly take a walk around the garden.

Fig 4 Paving patterns.

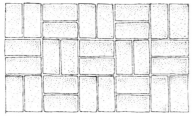

Basket weave

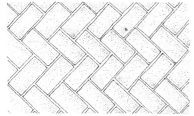

Herringbone (variation 1)

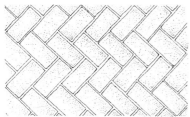

Herringbone (variation 2)

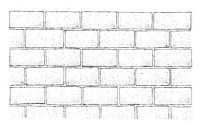

Coursed

Smaller units cope with curves

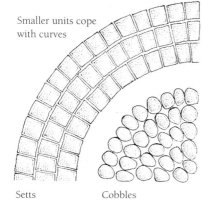

Setts   Cobbles

Alternative schemes for the garden were discussed, but this one was thought to be the simplest and the best. Diagonal and circular layout plans were rejected in favour of this balanced rectangularity, and the views from the house have justified this decision as the formal, square box 'parterres', symmetrically bordered on either side, pave the way to a raised 'stage' on which the summerhouse is central.

MATERIALS Beside the house, the courtyard is paved with real York stone, but it is aged and weathered, not new, as in the previous garden. This means the flagstones are darker and marked with use, and they have an air of belonging – as the area is very sunny there is no need for pale-coloured stone. Old frostproof bricks are laid in a 'chevron' pattern between the parterres, pointing the way forward. No cut-and-shaped bricks neaten the edges, so they merge well into the box hedging and meandering border plants. The colours of both paving and brickwork are muted and 'natural'. Contrast of colour has been avoided, as the different textures and patterns are sufficient. As a rule, if texture and materials are varied it would only irritate the eye if there were a colour contrast as well.

Permanent seats, one of stone beside the steps and one of cast iron beneath the pergola, offer alternative invitations to sit out in full sunshine, as seen in the photograph on page 36. The summerhouse, on the other hand, is sited in the shady end of the garden, and from this tranquil and dark cocoon the garden is displayed in bright sunlight, producing a quite different frame of mind.

THE PLANTING On either side of the garden the plant groups are always in contrast, as one border is mostly shaded and has correspondingly softly coloured plants, whereas the opposite side offers more opportunity for colour, aided and abetted by silver and grey foliage. Quite a lot of evergreens maintain the garden's structure all year round. Apart from the box, viburnums, small pines, *Mahonia x media* 'Winter Sun', two choisyas, bamboo, berberis and ferns keep the garden attractive throughout the seasons.

Since all the garden plants have to work overtime, as they always do in a small garden, it was decided that the best way to tackle the four matching boxed squares was to fill them with spring bulbs like *Narcissus* 'February Gold' and glory-of-the-snow (*Chionodoxa luciliae*), followed by squills (*Scilla*), lily-flowered tulips and other bulbs, all eventually to be replaced by summer annuals. In this way the squares can be beautiful throughout most of the year. The photographs show that in this particular year pink dianthus met the need for colour, but they will be removed and passed on, vacating the role for others.

Opposite: Gardens in towns fulfil many purposes; not only do they have to be beautiful but they must also be extensions of living space. The transition from conservatory to courtyard shown here is comfortable and inviting.

Around the squares, where the brickwork leads into the hedging, the owner has planted some small alpines and mat thymes quite randomly, thus pursuing an informal planting scheme within the strictly geometric symmetry.

At the far end, the fully shaded garden around the summerhouse is greatly affected by the conditions. Here *Euphorbia robbiae*, *Brunnera macrophylla* 'Hadspen Cream', *Pulmonaria angustifolia* 'Mawson's Variety' and large solomon's seal are assisted by white foxgloves and some *Lilium martagon* in summer. Ground covers like *Galax urceolata*, *Waldesteinia ternata*, *Lamium maculatum* 'Beacon Silver' and the lesser periwinkle *Vinca minor* all add glints of occasional colour. The area is damp enough to support small evergreen azaleas, but is bone dry beside the wall, and yet even here pyracantha does very well and a *Hydrangea petiolaris* is thriving.

Problems have occurred with climbing roses and honeysuckles in the garden. Mildew threatens, as so often in protected walled gardens, and has been causing trouble. In view of this the honeysuckles may go and some of the roses may be changed. However, *Cytisus battandieri* does well and *Jasminum officinale* 'Aureum' is very content. The deep red, scented *Rosa* 'Guinée' has also been trouble free, as it usually is.

This garden is constantly in flux and probably always will be. It has to please for twelve months of the year and cope with changes of light and shade as the tree canopy is reduced. These are typical small-garden requirements, but are not major problems.

CASE STUDY

A Garden in Three Units

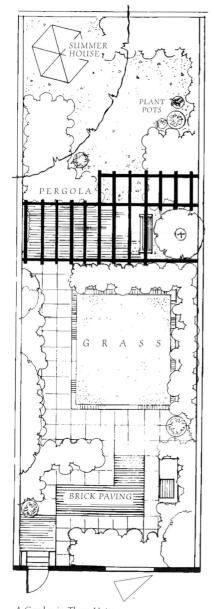

A Garden in Three Units
L-shaped rectangular spaces make this a
particularly pleasing design.

This small, recently completed garden is another urban plot on which many demands will be made.

THE LAYOUT Faced with a long, narrow site, the designer, Elizabeth Whateley, chose to divide it into three units. The first, near the house, is the largest and will be the most used. Here she has provided an easily managed paved area, partly enclosed by planting, which leads out on to a formal, brick-edged, neat lawn. The view from the house is therefore green and fringed all round with planting.

At the far end of this area, the garden is contained by a decisive timber pergola which crosses at right angles from one fence to the other. Part of this acts as an open screen, providing views into the third space, while to the left of these verticals is an entrance and here the path leads invitingly through into a canopied and secluded arbour. A less imaginative plan might have used hedging to establish the garden divisions, but the designer has retained an inviting glimpse of the third garden, as well as using the pergola as an opportunity to create a small, brick-paved, semi-shaded seating area underneath. This is a place with its own identity where a seat, enfolded by an old *Sorbaria aitchisonii*, befits its elegant surroundings. Once the canopy of wisteria and roses is established this will be an inviting and quiet space for repose.

Skillfully forming an L-shape at one end, the pergola leads on to the third garden. It has an existing summerhouse and is gravelled throughout.

As the site is only 7m (23ft) wide but 25m (82ft) long, sectioning it into three compartments and making paths which lead widthways as well as forward counters the difficult proportions, and makes this into an elegant and manageable garden.

THE PLANTING Intelligent planting, which is good-looking all seasons, adds to the sophisticated set. Shrubs like *Garrya elliptica* 'James Roof', *Viburnum davidii*, *Chaenomeles superba* 'Jet Trail', Cotoneaster *horizontalis*, *Abelia grandiflora*, *Carpenteria californica* and *Cistus ladanifer* add to the established shrubs. Massed over the pergola are four *Rosa* 'Adelaide D'Orleans' with *Clematis viticella* weaving through and *Vitis viniferapurpurea* adding greyish-purple tones that turn to crimson in autumn. There are climbers of distinction on the boundary fences.

The herbaceous planting adds colour and texture and most of the plants are very easy to maintain. Amongst them are old faithfuls like *Geranium* 'Johnson's Blue' and *Iris foetidissima* 'Citrina', plus some *Verbena bonariensis*, *Omphalodes cappadocica*, *Iris pallida pallida*, *Anemone japonica* 'Honorine Jobert', *Rudbeckia* 'Goldsturm' and *Helleborus argutifolius*, which create seasonal changes.

All three of the gardens discussed in this chapter are basically very simple. The angularity suits the city scene and they are easy to use as well as easy on the eye.

3 · Shamelessly Romantic

'The past is an important source of inspiration, but we still have to select what we like or indeed have space to include.'

As visiting great gardens has become so popular, many of us fill our heads with extravagantly large visions of the flower power of summer, redolent with scents and joyously romantic. But if we have small spaces we have to confine ourselves to the possible and work with what we have. The romance of flowers, bowers and secret areas can, however, be adapted if your scheme relates to your space. You may have seen features in these large and beautiful gardens which will provide the inspiration for your own design – your imagination is the key, and if it has been aroused by what you have seen, then you will want to make your own garden full of romantic appeal.

So what constitutes a romantic garden? Nostalgia certainly plays a part. Using traditional materials; reusing second-hand materials like brick; filling a garden with urns, classical arbours, traditional trellis and pergolas of brick and cedar; creating hidden spaces (think of the romance of the 'secret garden'); harking back to pools with fountains; forming follies, grottos and sundials; bridging water; making gazebos – all of these are features with echoes of times past and a quality of reassuring familiarity which neither challenges nor startles but is nonetheless romantic.

NOSTALGIA FOR PAST TIMES

As a means of deciding how to plan a small romantic garden, it is worth looking at some of the gardens of history. Time lends great charms to these and it is easy to forget how labour intensive they may have been. However, in the small garden, this will be reasonably manageable.

We look back to Shakespearean images of flowery 'meades', of roses and rosemary, lilies and lavender, all of which have overtones of arcadian tradition. The idea of herbs and knot gardens, so loved by the Elizabethans and popular in France and Italy, is today easily adaptable for the inward-looking smaller garden.

Fig 1 (opposite) shows a plan for an Italianate garden which has been planned around a cast-iron and glass loggia. The box hedging is intended to restrain the luxuriant planting around the courtyard. A centrally sited small fountain is fringed with white irises, scillas and *Thymus lanuginosa*. Other mat thymes, like *Thymus serpyllum* varieties and *Thymus* 'Anderson's Gold' are planted in spaces between the stone slabs and cobbles, both of which are local materials. The charisma of this intimate garden view lies in its associations with the past, yet it is not too difficult to manage as the box hedging creates boundaries.

Fig 1 Plan and elevation for a romantic garden.

Right: The plan shows an 'Italianate' design working well with the existing loggia. It was decided to relate the whole garden to the loggia, which is central to the window of the garden room, rather than to the framework of the house. A large paved area with permanent stone seats and a central raised small pool creates a tranquil space amongst lush planting. Existing shrubs were retained and are shown on the plan.

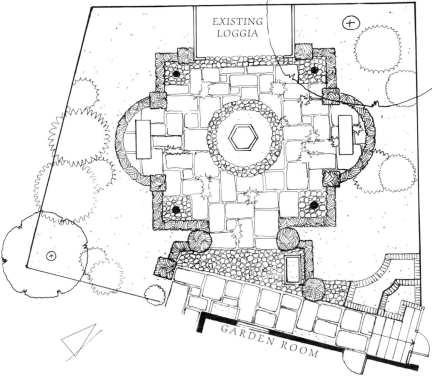

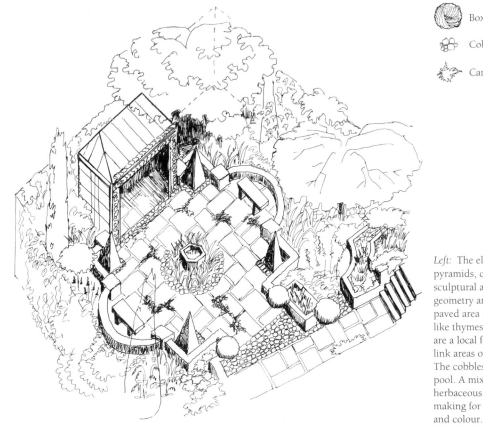

Box hedging

Cobbles

Carpet plants

Left: The elevation shows simple topiary of pyramids, cubes and domes that are sculptural and static. They reinforce the geometry and balance the design. The large paved area is softened with carpet plants like thymes, *Raoulia* and *Acaena*. Cobbles are a local feature and have been used to link areas of paving that are not in parallel. The cobbles also frame the topiary and the pool. A mixture of trees, shrubs and herbaceous plants surrounds the area, making for rich patterns of form, texture and colour.

PERGOLAS, ARCHES AND ARBOURS

Pergolas and arches feature in the romance of bygone ages. In the past, traditional pergolas were almost tunnels, rather reminiscent of cloisters, sometimes created on a frame and at other times by manipulating trees like hornbeam or lime to construct the forms themselves. Practical training of fruit trees, laburnum or even Portuguese laurel on metal arches can eventually create tunnels. Depending upon the chosen climber, the light intensity within the closed alley can vary from dappled to very dark indeed. On the whole, modern pergolas tend to be more modest affairs, where either metal hooped arches or timber piers and lintels create alternative shapes, as seen in Fig 2.

For centuries the vine has continued to be an ideal plant for pergolas. Obviously, there were functional reasons for this originally, but it is also a most decorative plant. *Vitis vinifera* 'Purpurea', the Teinturier grape, is a most beautiful climber, with soft claret red/greyish foliage which turns a glowing crimson in the fall. The golden hop, *Humulus lupulus* 'Aureus,' is also strikingly coloured, with large yellow leaves. Rambling and climbing roses, clematis and honeysuckle, all appropriate to the romantic garden, can wend their way up pergolas, providing light or dense cover, scents and screening. The plant list opposite explains the different contributions made by rambling and climbing roses.

Arbours, traditionally made from timber or grown within strong hedges, are places for introspection. The overhead cover, like that of the pergola, is mainly of living plants, supported on the frame. Arbours act as romantic focal points within the design of the garden, as well as transitional places where movement pauses and there is time for the quality of life, thinking or reading and, of course, romance. Some ideas for construction are shown in Fig 3 (opposite). An arbour can be quite small – in scale with your garden – and be an excellent substitute for a summerhouse.

SUMMERHOUSES AND GAZEBOS

Small buildings outside featured very early in garden history and they too serve as much for romantic style as for function. The early influences were from cultures as far apart as loggias in ancient Rome, Chinese pavilions and Mogul temples. In our small-garden terms, summerhouses or gazebos, usually timber built, can add the same charm as those of the past, but on a different scale.

HISTORICAL FURNISHINGS

Detail is important when creating gardens of the past. This is why there are so many successful companies making reproductions in wood, concrete, metal and resin with glass fibre. Versailles tubs, Gothic seats, Renaissance Italian stone benches, porch seats from Virginia, Chinese Chippendale furniture, wirework tables, lead tanks and Lutyens chairs, not to mention sundials, obelisks, urns, amphoras and vases, are all readily available. Some refer back as far as classical Greece, while others belong to different cultures and periods in history.

Fig 2 Pergolas and arches.

A formal pergola with substantial brick piers supporting a timber frame. Large climbers like wisteria, hops, *Vitis coignetiae* and heavy rambling roses suit this well.

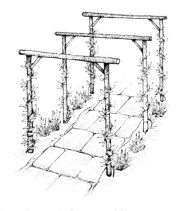

A smaller rustic frame would carry traditional climbers like honeysuckles, clematis and scented roses.

A metal arch could be used to train fruit trees, vines or *Laburnum*.

These furnishings can be most attractive in intimate gardens, where detail is so noticeable. Being stylish in their own right, they act as decorative ornaments as well as serving functional roles. Reproductions of statuary can also be purchased (though personally I am none too keen on half-sized Venus de Milos). Some are antiques and can be worth a great deal of money if made from expensive materials like lead or Coade stone. Otherwise, take care if choosing reproduction work. It can be made from badly cast concrete with air holes and thick seams, and it is worth paying extra for the more finely cast items, which can pass for more natural materials. Figurative work can be very clumsy and deformed in the casting process, so it too needs examining thoroughly.

All such features add an air of romance to a garden, particularly when 'aged' with lichen, half covered in ivy or semi-concealed in shaded areas. However, we cannot have everything. The past is an important source of inspiration, but we still have to select what we like or indeed have space to include.

Fig 3 Arbours.

A timber-framed open arbour.

Metal bowers can be covered with rambling roses.

CLIMBING AND RAMBLING ROSES

Rambling roses are either species roses or allied garden forms. They can be lax in habit or pliant, enabling them to be curved over arches or up into trees. Most flower only once but with an excellent display.
Climbing roses tend to be stiffer in habit. They may be old shrub roses which grow tall or modern climbers. They usually have large flowers and often flower continuously.

Recommended climbers

Aimée Vibert – Small white clusters, continuous flowering, shade tolerant
Bantry Bay – Pink, repeat flowering
Blairi No 2 – Pale pink, fragrant, repeat flowering
Chaplin's Pink – Bright pink, summer flowering
Compassion – Apricot, fragrant, repeat flowering
Dublin Bay – Crimson, fragrant, continuous flowering
Etoile de Hollande – Crimson, fragrant, continuous flowering, shade tolerant
Gloire de Dijon – Salmon, fragrant, continuous flowering, shade tolerant
Guinée – Dark red, fragrant, summer flowering plus a few, shade tolerant
Handel – White edged red, fragrant, repeat flowering
Iceberg (climbing) – White, summer flowering, shade tolerant
Josephine Bruce (climbing) – Dark red, summer flowering
Lady Hillingdon – Apricot, fragrant, repeat flowering

Madame Alfred Carrière – White, fragrant, repeat flowering, shade tolerant
Madame Gregoire Staechelin – Strong pink, fragrant, early flowering, shade tolerant
Meg – Apricot, single, repeat flowering
Mermaid – Yellow, single, fragrant, repeat flowering
New Dawn – Pale pink, fragrant, repeat flowering
Pink Perpétue – Deep pink, continuous flowering
Rêve d'Or – Buff/yellow, fragrant, repeat flowering
Schoolgirl – Copper/orange, fragrant, repeat flowering
Swan Lake – White, repeat flowering
Zepherine Drouhin – Rose pink, fragrant, repeat flowering

Recommended ramblers

Adelaide d'Orleans – Powder pink, scented, summer flowering
Alberic Barbier – Cream/yellow, scented, summer flowering, shade tolerant
Albertine – Copper-pink, summer flowering
Alister Stella Gray – Yellow, scented, repeat flowering, shade tolerant
Emily Grey – Yellow, fragrant, summer flowering, shade tolerant
Félicité et Perpétue – Cream/white, fragrant, midsummer flowering
Francis E. Lester – Pink/white, fragrant, summer flowering
Phyllis Bide – Yellow/salmon, repeat flowering
Veilchenblau – Magenta/blue/violet, scented, summer flowering, shade tolerant

A timber frame with trellis encloses a seat.

An imposing trellised arbour to create dappled shade.

An elegant white seat within clipped yew.

This romantic pool is actually uncompromisingly geometric, with its long, narrow shape. It is the beautiful border planting of pink sidalcea and maroon alliums linking back and forth across the water that make this such a charming picture.

POOLS

Water must be mentioned within the context of the romantic garden. Usually formally planned on traditional lines, the styles of pools can vary, and a few classical pool shapes are shown in Fig 4 (opposite). On the other hand, the simple rectangular form is hard to beat. In the past, some large classical gardens included long canal-like structures of water wherein the smooth surface was romantically reflective. In the photograph above the long, slim pool is calmly beautiful, graced with flowers and foliage along its length. It is just a simple, narrow rectangle but is far from ordinary as it is so well furnished with plants.

Should you wish to include moving water, such as a fountain, this will become the most dominant part of the garden, so it should be planned

Fig 4 Simple geometric shapes make attractive formal pools.

with care and in scale with the space. A gentle trickle or splash can be refreshing and pleasantly soothing, but some fountains sound like faulty water cisterns, which is far from romantic.

Practical considerations are important when designing any waterworks in a garden. You need to site it carefully: the ecological balance is achieved more easily if the pool has at least five hours of sunlight each day in cooler climates, as shade tends to make water brackish if it is not moving. Deciding, too, whether to agitate the water or keep it smooth and still will affect your plant choices. It is as well also to work out the ratio of surface area to depth, as this can be calculated to maintain the balanced health of plants and fish. The bibliography on page 140 suggests some excellent books on the subject of pools and expert advice is well worth observing.

GARDENS OF MOOD

Romantics do not always look to the past. Mood gardens can be in a modern idiom where flowing gravel, timber decks and concrete flagstones create a different look. A sense of drama can be formed by half-concealed entrances to secret spaces, glimpses through trellis of half-explained features or gardens overwhelmed with flowers and draped with climbers.

If you know that this is the feeling of garden you want, there are different ways of achieving it. Surprisingly, the layout could be quite formal and designed on a grid basis, where overflowing foliage and flower dominate everything. Claude Monet's garden at Giverny in France is a good example of this. It has a very wide central-axis path, over which lax stems of nasturtiums trail in summer, while parallel paths lead off on either side at right angles. There is also a second garden which is quite different. This one is not grid rigid, but is made from flowing abstract shapes around the informal curves of a pond. A Japanese style of arched bridge carries wisteria above head height over the water, and nothing could be more romantic.

As already mentioned, the structural pattern in the main garden is unexpectedly severe, but acts as a strong format upon which the most excitingly coloured plants drift around each other. Wide, trellised arches span the paths, carrying the planting extravaganza overhead with wisteria, clematis and rambling roses. Annually, poppies, forget-me-nots, marguerites, pansies, marigolds and corncockles fill spaces between structured verticals of roses, tulips, hollyhocks and delphiniums. It is colour which motivates rather than the plants themselves. The endless changing of light quality fascinated this painter of light and colour. From this garden one can move on to the pool garden beyond, where there are no straight lines or right-angled junctions. Paths and plants meander in random curves around the large, flat water surface and the much-painted lily pads lie horizontally inert on the pool, creating a scene of harmony and tranquillity.

Left: Overflowing pinks, powder blues and lilacs add great romance to the rustic arches. Nepeta, viola and delphiniums provide the blues and *Rosa* 'Comte de Chambord' is heavy with highly scented quartered rosette flowers.

Above: An archway flanked by luminous clematis and pink roses leads through invitingly to a sunlit summer garden beyond.

What can we learn from this? The two layouts are very different, but both gardens have a single purpose: colour and textures dominate, making both garden forms subservient. What they have in common is the flowing vitality of the plants, counterbalanced either by the formally structured layout in the first garden, or by the spacious, smooth surface of the water in the second. The 'yin-yang' balance of opposites is why both gardens work so well. The photograph above shows an entrance to the garden.

FEATURES

Gardens of the emotions do not dictate a style of furnishings. Certainly a rusticity is possible, where wattle may figure and arches, trellis and seats can be made from sawn larch or chestnut poles. The simplicity of this style probably has its origins in romantic ideas of hermits and rural life, and many people choose it today in preference to highly finished or painted timber structures.

If well done, rustic work can have an honest simplicity which is most welcome in a small garden, as in the photograph opposite of a rustic pergola planted with roses and nepeta by Wendy Lauderdale. However, rustic imagery can also smack of gnomery, if on too small a scale, with over-narrow arches and if tacked together insubstantially.

Similarly, cast-iron seats or tables can also be over-elaborate, so that metallic scrolls and plant patterns vie with living, twisting, floriferous growth. Competition between objects and plants produces weakened design: one should flatter the other, and there should never be a fight for attention. Either the feature is large enough or sufficiently sculpturally dominant to make the planting subservient, or the feature is quietly well behaved and modestly settles within glorious planting.

'NATURAL' POOLS

Informal, 'natural' pools have special charm today as people are so ecology-sensitive. It is not a new idea. Water has been trained to fulfil man's needs since ancient Egyptian times, and the tradition spread from agriculture to garden culture. Small fish-stocked ponds with lotus or lilies were forerunners of the large artificial lakes made to enhance grand landscapes. Today, it is relatively simple to make a 'natural' pond in a small garden. Either waterproofed concrete or heavy butyl plastic liners can be used, but the latter is easiest for random shapes as was mentioned in Chapter 1. This type of pond has sloping sides so that it merges well with poolside planting. It does not necessarily have to be completely natural, with 'wild' bog plants like most of those in Chapter 1, but can be very successful if associated with bamboo, reeds, grasses, ferns, ligularia, astilbes, hostas, marsh marigolds (*Caltha*) and so forth. Most of these are garden plants – the lusher the planting the more romantic the scene.

If your plot is extremely small then this could well be the only feature and, should this be the case, either randomly shaped stone slabs beside the water, or crisp decking overhanging it, would make a seating area in character with the rural style of the pool. Or perhaps an edging of gravel, graded up to pebble size to make a beach, would also make the water look attractively natural. However, if small children are likely to spend any unaccompanied time in the garden no water feature is to be recommended, apart from a fountain which falls on to a draining surface where there is no depth of water. Pools are hazardous.

Informal pools are shown in Fig 5. One uses decking and the other irregularly shaped rocks.

THE ROMANCE OF PLANTS

For gardens in which dreams are made, flowers are the essence of romance, although lush foliage backdrops, twining climbers, a light tree canopy, fragrances and rustles are all very significant. But the flowers themselves are probably the first thought.

ROSES AND ASSOCIATES

Roses must be to the forefront in the romantic-style garden. Rambling, climbing, shrub and patio roses offer great ranges of size and form. The colours are sometimes a little garish, but these are often the result of hybridization – for example, the flower colour of 'Masquerade' is crude when compared with that of *Rosa chinesis* 'Mutabilis', but this is of course my own personal preference. Do note that these two roses are also quite

Fig 5 Informal pools.

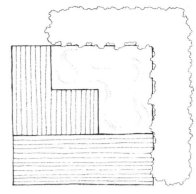

Timber decking overhanging a rectangular pool.

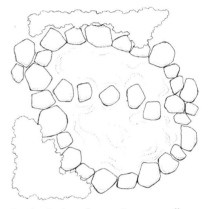

Randomly shaped stones integrate well as edging and as stepping stones for an informal pool.

SMALLER SHRUB ROSES

Ballerina – Pink/white, 1.2m (4ft)
The Fairy – Pink, small clusters, repeat flowering, 1m (3ft)
Golden Wings – Yellow, continuous flowering, 1.2m (4ft)
Graham Thomas – Yellow, fragrant, continuous flowering, 1.2m (4ft)
Heritage – Shell pink, continuous flowering, 1.2m (4ft)
Kassel – Scarlet, continuous flowering, 1m (3ft)
Kent – White, semi-double, large trusses, summer flowering, 60cm (2ft)
Pink Bells – Pink, summer flowering, 1.2m (4ft)
Queen Mother – Pink, 60cm (2ft)
Rutland – Pink, small clusters, repeat flowering, 30cm (1ft)
Surrey – Rose-pink, double, continuous flowering, 60cm (2ft)
Warwickshire – Red/white, single flowers, perpetual flowering, 45cm (1½ft)

OLD SHRUB ROSES
Many old shrub roses can be very tall and invasive.

Alba
Königin von Dänemark – Pink, fragrant
Maiden's Blush – Pale pink, fragrant
Bourbon
Boule de Neige – White, fragrant
Souvenir de la Malmaison – Pale pink, fragrant
Centifolia
Fantin Latour – Pale pink
Rose de Meaux – Small, deep pink
William Lobb – Purple/red
Chinensis
Old Blush China – Pink
Perle d'Or – Yellow/apricot
Damask
Comte de Chambord – Pink, fragrant
Madame Hardy – White, fragrant
Gallica
Camaieux – Striped white/crimson, fragrant
Charles de Mills – Cerise/purple, fragrant
Rosa mundi – Crimson, striped white
Hybrid Musk
Buff Beauty – Apricot/yellow/buff
Penelope – Pink/salmon/yellow, hips
Cornelia – Pink/copper/apricot
Hybrid Perpetual
Ferdinand Pichard – Striped red/white
Souvenir de Dr Jamain – Plum/purple/red, fragrant
Rugosa (bushy and dense)
Agnes – Apricot, parsley leaves
Frau Dagmar Hartopp – Pale pink, scented, hips
Pink Grootendorst – Frilled pink, continuous flowering
Species (Can be tall; usually small single flowers)
R. chinensis 'Mutabilis' – Copper/yellow/pink, tall, best on a wall, 1.5m (5ft)
R. moyesii 'Geranium' – Single red flowers, red hips, 2.4m (8ft)
R. primula – Early, single yellow, scented foliage, 1.5m (5ft)
R. rubrifolia – Grey foliage, 1.8m (6ft)
R. woodsii fendleri – Lilac/pink flowers, good hips, 1.5m (5ft)

different in form, the first being a bush 90cm (3ft) tall while the second reaches 2.4m (8ft) and, being lax, grows better on a warm wall.

Old garden roses have names which are as romantic as their appearance, such as musk, moss and damask. These older roses mostly flower once in early summer, but due to their arching elegance and often densely pretty foliage they merge easily with other summer plants, and the traditional associations with paeonies, alchemilla, irises, geraniums and pinks are glorious. Many of them are very old, like the albas and gallicas, both of which are scented. Some are species with origins from around the world. These mostly have small single flowers and very attractive hips.

Modern shrub roses have been bred for the best characteristics of the old and also for a longer flowering period and disease resistance, so in the small garden these have extra worth. Among the best are 'Buff Beauty', which is an old-gold and parchment colour; 'Felicia', a silvery-pink scented rose; and 'Penelope', equally fragrant, palely salmon-pink and recurrent flowering. Some of the old roses have double or quartered form like 'Königin von Dänemark', an elegant pink alba rose. This quartering is not characteristic of the modern roses, previously known as hybrid tea and now as large-flowered. The latter were mainly bred for the purity of single flowerheads and to produce specimens like those sold by florists when 'a dozen red roses' are ordered. Among the old roses there are rich crimson-purple flowers like those of 'Souvenir de Dr Jamain', a highly scented hybrid perpetual, or white ones such as 'Madame Hardy', a nineteenth-century damask rose. Some have extraordinary names like 'Wolley Dod's Rose' syn. 'Pomifera Duplex', which is a semi-double pink, or 'Chapeau de Napoleon', an unusual centifolia. Should you become interested in roses it could easily become an absorbing passion: the history and variety of the rose is endlessly fascinating, and the list on these pages suggests just some.

Many shrub roses are bare at the base, but this is easily solved with flattering grey foliage plants like *Stachys lanata*, *Santolina chamaecyparissus* and the lower-growing artemisias. Amongst other plants which carry the romantic allusion are lavender, nepeta, hollyhocks, lilies, violas, poppies, verbascum, irises and campanulas – and this list could be greatly expanded. In spring, snowdrops, daffodils, bluebells and primroses carry the same gentle associations.

COLOUR

To create glorious planting without also making a messy multi-coloured *mélange*, it is necessary to link the colours together. Without going into the detail of colour theory, it is useful to know that some colours are near to one another in the spectrum, like red-orange-yellow and blue-lilac-purple, and thus some natural harmony occurs. Consequently, you can create planting patterns of reds, yellows and oranges or blues, lilacs and purples and these will be effective. They will also be referred to as 'hot' or 'cool' borders, because colour is also perceived as suggesting temperature change. Fun can be had by clashing one hot colour within a cool border; for example, tulips of a warm red amongst blue forget-me-nots. Then, there are what are termed 'complementary' relationships. This is when colours which are 'opposite' one another in the colour 'wheel' bring out the best and the worst in each other. This is actually quite a complicated concept, as there are many other implications; but to simplify, red and green, blue and orange, and yellow and purple are all paired opposites which act in this way. The three first-named colours – red, blue and yellow – are all known as 'primary' colours because they are pure hues which cannot be made from any others, whereas the three 'secondaries' – green, orange and purple – are created by mixing two of the primary colours, such as blue and yellow to make green, red and yellow to make orange, and red and blue to make purple. Each primary has its complement, or 'opposite', secondary colour as described.

When both the primary and its complementary are of equal 'value', that is equal strength, the relationship is very dramatic: for example, the much-used combination of yellow alyssum with purple aubrieta is very popular. Though not exact opposites, the purple of the aubrieta veers towards blue, but these are strong colours together and I am not very keen on the combination. I prefer to change the relationship by using the paler *Alyssum saxatile* 'Citrinum' with the deeply purple *Aubrieta* 'Dr Mules'. What has happened here is that by selecting a lighter shade of yellow the purple becomes the dominant colour, so that the two colours are no longer of equal value and do not engage in combat.

This leads on to the other main influencing factor when choosing colour combinations: beyond consideration of primary and secondary colours, there is also a limitless variety of tints and tones. There are darks, pastels, and many in between. Just by selecting a paler version, for example, a colour can vastly improve its relationship within the border. The main aim should be to avoid a 'riot of colour', where each colour is equal in intensity and clamouring for attention.

This is a complicated subject, as any painter or designer will tell you. Nevertheless, in terms of the romantic garden you have already limited your choices, which should help. Pastel shades will predominate, with occasional flashes of vivid hues to activate a scene. Dark shades create depths, which add mystery as well as being foils for lighter groups. It is worth noting that white and pale blue are particularly lustrous in shade, as will be noticed in the evening. Probably the most romantic colour associations are pinks, lilacs, blues, creams and whites, often in association with silvery-grey foliage.

The photograph opposite above shows a white rose over a white picket gate with a white house beyond. The colour range is extremely restricted but quite beautiful. Compare it with the very charming scene of a cottage garden (opposite below) where shades of pink are dominant. The pink rose rules the colour scheme but foxgloves (*Digitalis purpurea*) and valerian (*Centranthus ruber*) add strong shades, and a honeysuckle with cream and pinkish-purple flowers lifts the colour.

SCENED SHRUBS

Aromatic foliage

Clerodendron bungei
Escallonia
Helichrysum plicatum
Hyssopus officinalis
Lavandula
Lindera
Lippia citriodora
Myrica gale
Myrtus communis
Olearia
Ptelea
Rosa primula
Rosmarinus officinalis
Santolina
Skimmia laureola

Scented flowers

Camellia sasanqua
Chimonanthus praecox
Choisya ternata
Cytisus battandieri
Daphne
Deutzia
Hamamelis mollis 'Brevipetala' and others
Jasminum humile 'Revolutum'
Lonicera fragrantissima
L. x purpusii
Magnolia
Mahonia japonica
M. x media 'Charity'
Olearia odorata
Osmanthus delavayi
Philadelphus
Poncirus trifoliata
Rhododendron azaleas
Rosa
Sarcococca hookeriana var. *humilis*
Syringa
Viburnum

White gardens can be just as romantic as pink and blue ones, as this picture shows. The charming white picket gate is emphasized by an arch of white climbing roses and leads to a white house beyond. The whole scene is enhanced by silver foliage.

Compare the cool purity of the white planting above with the warm colour surrounding this old red-brick house. The vibrant colours of honeysuckle and roses adorn the house wall, while poppies, valerian, campanula, phlox, achillea and foxgloves merge beautifully as traditional cottage garden plants.

FOLIAGE PLANTS

Combining plants to best effect involves using their size, shape and foliage to blend harmoniously with the great variety of greens which are the mainstay of any garden. Greens vary from lime to jade to emerald and to nearly black. Textured surfaces can be glossy, puckered, woolly or matt, affecting the 'value' of the hue: it will be more intense when glossy and paler if hairy. Silver foliage like that of the artemisias, santolinas, stachys and some salvias also acts as a foil in a flower border. All these different patterns can create wonderful effects, but to avoid a foliage farrago always select with care. Too much of everything will 'gild the lily' and all is lost in chaos.

One can aim to control this *omnium gatherum* by deploying clear shapes. These are plants which provide definition of form; that is, amongst the great vitality of herbaceous flowers, the key to displaying them well is to have some simple shapes against which they are seen. The classic clipped dark yew hedge, brick wall, or solid and dense forms of plants like clipped box or Portuguese laurel, have a strength against which the daisy flowers, the hazy flowers, the stately, the elegant and the pretty are shown at their best. Single forms can be powerfully effective, be they Irish juniper (*Juniperus communis* 'Hibernica') a fastigiate yew (*Taxus baccata* 'Fastigiata') or rounded hebes and strongly shaped *Prunus laurocerasus* varieties like 'Otto Luyken' or 'Zabeliana'. Dramatic foliage forms like the cardoon (*Cynara cardunculus*), *Phormium tenax*, *Euphorbia wulfenii* and humbler irises, sisyrinchium, kniphofia and hostas also provide structured control points amongst the flowers. A really successful mixed bed of herbaceous perennials can be photographed with black and white film and still be stunning, as the shapes and textures will be evident.

SIZE

Relative size must obviously be considered, as plants should be encouraged to weave in and out of each other's mass. Presenting a tidy line of 'small at the front' grading up to 'tall at the back' is regimental rather than romantic. Using large forms to distinguish plants from mass decoration is a great help. For example, *Sambucus racemosa* 'Plumosa Aurea' is a mass of yellow; *Mahonia x media* 'Winter Sun' is a tall sculpture; *Choisya ternata* makes a glossy rounded mound; and some of the hydrangeas and viburnums form horizontal patterns with their lacecap flowers. These provide large architectural forms against which other, more intricate plants look particularly pretty.

Climbers are a means of taking plants well above eye level and are invaluable in the romantic scene. Roses can ramble up walls, over pergolas or into trees; clematis can drape themselves upon others; honeysuckles may loop in swags from one pier to another – the movement of climbers can envelop the garden, adding texture with colour, and very many of them are scented as well. The photograph opposite shows a garden belonging to Wendy Lauderdale, who planned

CLIMBING PLANTS FOR PERGOLAS

Evergreens
Aristolochia sempervirens
Clematis armandii
C. cirrhosa balearica
Escallonias (shrub)
Hedera canariensis 'Gloire de Marengo'
H. colchica 'Dentata'
H. c. 'Dentata Aurea'
H. c. 'Sulphur Heart' (syn. 'Paddy's Pride')
Hedera helix 'Angularis Aurea' (training required)
H. h. 'Atropurpurea' (training required)
H. h. 'Buttercup' (training required)
H. h. 'Goldheart' (training required)
Lonicera henryi
Lonicera japonica 'Aureoreticulata'
L. j. 'Halliana' (rampant)

Deciduous
Actinidia kolomitka (training required)
Aristolochia macrophylla (training required)
Campsis x tagliabuana 'Madame Galen'
Clematis
Eccremocarpus scaber
Humulus lupulus 'Aurea'
Jasminum officinale f. *affine*
Lonicera vars
Parthenocissus henryana
Passiflora caerulea
P. 'Exoniensis'
Rosa climbers and ramblers
Solanum crispum 'Glasnevin'
S. jasminoides 'Album'
Vitis cognetiae
V. vinifera 'Aplifolia'
V. v. 'Brandt'
V. v. 'Incana'
V. v. 'Purpurea'

Scented climbers
Clematis armandii
C. cirrhosa balearica
Jasminum officinale f. *Affine*
Lonicera
Rosa
Trachelospermum
Vitis riparia
Wisteria

This beautiful garden seen in high summer was planned and planted by Wendy Lauderdale. Redolent with scents we can only imagine, blue foliage of *Ruta graveolens* and dark red *Rosa bleu magenta* add great vitality to the scene.

it and grew the plants herself. Climbing roses like 'Wedding Day' and 'Bantry Bay', footed by pale blue nepeta, link the other plants which are mainly white, pinks and blues. Regrettably, the photograph cannot show the fragrance of the white climbing rose.

GARDENS OF THE SENSES

One of the great pleasures in gardens is non-visual, and scent is much sought after in all gardens, not just those of romantic character. The small garden has to work hard to fulfil so many needs, but fragrance is high in priority. As well as the summer scents of roses, pinks, lavenders, jasmine, honeysuckle and so forth, there are winter scents which are a joy for being so unexpected. Amongst these do consider *Daphne mezereum*, *Chimonanthus praecox*, *Lonicera purpusii*, *Mahonia japonica* and, for warmer climes, *Camellia sasanqua*. It is well worth planning carefully so that scents are close to the house in all seasons. A list of aromatic foliage plants and fragrant flowers is provided on page 48.

GARDENS FOR ALL SEASONS

On the whole, the small romantic garden tends to be associated with summer. It is a garden style which is less easy to cope with on an all-year-round basis. However, the exuberance of the growing seasons can be stretched. Autumn bulbs, winter foliage and fruit can extend the colour range through the year until the daffodil season takes over. Herbaceous plants like *Liriope muscari*, ophiopogon, Japanese anemones, argyranthemum, michaelmas daisies, agapanthus, *Kniphofia uvaria*, liatris and *Sedum spectabile* are all still in flower in mid-autumn. Caryopteris, teuchrium, ceratostigma and the unusual *Argyranthemum laterifolius* add shades of blue for another month. *Nerine bowdenii*, Kaffir lily (*Schizostylis coccinea*), and old chrysanthemums like 'Empress of China' add pinks and red in late autumn, and *Aster tradescantii* only begins its white flowering at the eleventh hour, so to speak. Late-flowering clematis, like the viticella varieties and some of the yellow-flowered species, should not be forgotten and, given a kindly autumn, roses uncomplainingly continue to provide flowers, sometimes into early winter. Chinese lantern (*Physalis*) and honesty (*Lunaria annua*) provide strikingly delicate seedheads, all within the romantic picture, though both are territorially ambitious.

Eventually, beneath flowering mahonias, varieties of the hellebores, pulmonarias and celandines take over with occasional flowerings from *Iris unguicularis*, and then the series of spring bulbs begin to flower. The photograph opposite shows a classic composition of yellow lily-flowered tulips and forget-me-nots in spring. The rose is *Rosa hugonis*, amongst the earliest in the year to flower. Another rose, *Rosa primula*, which is also a shrub rose with small, single yellow flowers, performs almost as early and has incense-scented foliage.

For deep winter, the opportunities are obviously rather more restricted, depending upon your climatic zone. Yet there is nothing more romantic than frost-clothed winter shrubs in morning mist. Elegance of habit can be seen so well in winter when bare forms are revealed. Acers in particular create delicate linear patterns. Chaenomeles – quince – has a natural grace and is an asset when a specimen branch is cut for indoors. Trailing catkins of *Garrya elliptica* and racemes of *Stachyurus praecox* in late winter add further patterns of linear charm, reminiscent of the catkin-like flowers of the scented *Itea ilicifolia* which flowers in late summer.

Small trees chosen for their elegance of form can also be of great charm out of season. *Betula pendula* 'Tristis', *Acer japonicum* varieties, weeping ash and *Prunus subhirtella* 'Pendula' all possess a stylish habit. The weeping aspen, *Populus tremula* 'Pendula', carries trails of grey-purple catkins. However, the ultimate size must be considered within your own plot.

In some cases, trees can be chosen for their bark. The white bark of *Betula utilis* var. *jacquemontii* has been described in Chapter 1; there are other slim birches with attractive bark, but here again, check the ultimate

Spring colours of yellow and blue provide a welcome sight after the winter. The yellow of *Rosa hugonis,* one of the earliest flowering roses, is echoed in the gold flowers of the lily tulips, with forget-me-knots and bluebells at their feet.

height in case it is not suitable for your small space. *Acer griseum,* *A. davidii* and *Prunus serrula* are all justifiably well known for their bark, however, do bear in mind the spread as well as the height. This also applies to the violet willow, *Salix daphnoides,* and to the red or yellow stems of the cornus family.

Thus the romantic charm of the small garden can be spread over the seasons, but if you are dealing with a very small space indeed you may have to make a ruthless decision: whether or not to go all-out for summer impact and thereby draw the drapes over winter.

4 · User Friendly

'For some... gardening is not always the guiltless pleasure that it is for others.'

The traditional notion of gardening as a relaxed, leisurely activity is not entirely appropriate in many busy lives. Nature's pace is ignored, as many of us take on exacting schedules and set for ourselves standards of perfection which are not easily realized. For some, therefore, gardening is not always the guiltless pleasure that it is for others. We still want beautiful gardens but this does not mean that we can easily manage them.

In the past the ambitions and imagination of the wealthier classes knew no bounds. The lavishly huge gardens of royal France, the dramatically spacious gardens of Renaissance Italy and the glories of the English estates are now presenting vast and costly problems of restoration and maintenance. So, grateful as we are to visit these grand undertakings, our own ambitions are often restricted by funds, time and a lack of space. Inspiration can be sought, but our garden often has priorities which were rarely the concerns of the past.

The gardens in this chapter are therefore practical. Although this sounds rather sad, it need not be so. In each case the first requirement was for beauty. Phrases like 'not too costly', 'easily managed' or 'this must be appropriate for the family... and the dog', were added afterwards. First and foremost there was the same fundamental desire to enhance the surroundings which runs throughout garden history.

Contemporary gardening has had to adapt to lack of labour and adopt new, less labour-intensive methods. Garden centres offer equipment which can cut, shred and blow, while the traditional tools become elaborately specific so we need more of them. Good: I am all for saving labour. I have no nostalgia for washing clothes in the river and am only too pleased to throw a switch instead. Traditional gardening also demands time when it is not necessarily convenient for modern schedules, so that some gardens must be able to manage without us. Thus the gardens in this chapter have been made with function in mind. They suit the needs of the owner, are mostly easy to control, and are low in maintenance requirements. Nonetheless, first and foremost they are very attractive.

FIRST CONSIDERATIONS

So what are the practical priorities when considering your small garden, in order to make it efficient and functional for use and pleasure?

Firstly, you need to consider how it will be used and by whom. A garden for young children would be quite different from that planned for teenagers. Young children use wheels in the smallest spaces, as any harassed mother knows. Steps become a hazard, as do sunken drains and soft verges. Older children want barbecues large enough for an overwhelming number of friends. Elderly people must be absolutely sure of non-slip paved surfaces. Other requirements are for play equipment, clothes lines, storage tanks, refuse bins and, in this green society, at least two heaps of compost – one resting and one in use.

Some garden owners need space to sit eight, ten or more people outside for a meal, while others want only a small table and a couple of chairs. But a practical requirement which nearly everyone would like is a place to sit. Preferably this should be permanent, being built in, or allowance should be made for folding chairs, but definitely there must be room for sitting outside in a pleasant garden retreat – so the design of the garden must make provision for rest.

It is important to add that in the case of minimum horticultural activity a lot is expected of the hard landscaping. The materials used and the way they are put together should make life easier. In a kitchen the idea of a 'work triangle' is accepted; that is, the likely movement between sink, cooker and refrigerator can be anticipated. Ideally, for maximum efficiency between these three points the distance walked should not be over 6m (20ft) and it must be free of obstacles. Space must also be allowed for others to pass though without jeopardizing the needs of the cook. Areas for work surfaces, power points, storage and seating are all to be considered. Mundane though it sounds, practical planning of exactly the same kind is extremely important if the small garden is to be trouble free. How the garden is to be *used* must be taken into account at the planning stage.

STEPS

If there are complications of levels, aim to reduce the inconvenience of this by terracing. Steps are often an attractive feature. They will look more inviting if they are wide, and if so the heights of the risers should be kept below 12cm (5in). Wide steps look more comfortable to use and people need not file up them singly, thus interrupting the social flow. Sometimes, however, much narrower steps are necessary and these should be steeper, though the risers should still be no more than 17cm (7in) high.

The plan shows two alternative solutions for a fairly narrow but useable yard. In Fig 1 the basement leads to a 3.4m (11ft) wide space which is further narrowed by a 90cm (3ft) wide-brick retained planting bed along the boundary wall. The area is mostly used for people to circulate between the two living rooms and also provides access to the garden. The view from the French windows is particularly important. Fig 2 shows the alternative plan which was adopted. This provides a far more attractive view, as well as creating a greater feeling of width. By terracing the yard as well as the steps the effect of this as a sunken basement is no longer

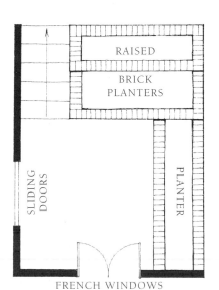

Fig 1 Before – Deeply sunken enclosed courtyard with narrow steps.

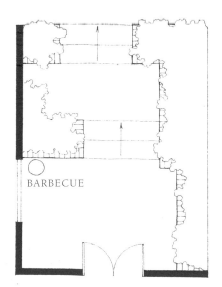

Fig 2 After – The same area is less confining when the levels are terraced and steps off-set.

55

emphasized. The area seems lighter and more pleasant. The planting prospect is also far better balanced. It is always worth giving thought to the planning of steps without necessarily going for the easiest option.

SURFACES

This courtyard is not intended for family use. The levels are too complicated for negotiation by toddlers who will lug large plastic toys around with them. Safety has to be an issue, as does accessibility. Attractive as they may be, brick pavers are not ideal for small children as the surface can become uneven and the bricks themselves slippery with algae. A roughened non-slip surface of precast flagstones or concrete stretch with exposed aggregate will provide sufficient friction for safe use.

PAVING

Real paving slabs are beautiful and come in many shades. Some are to be avoided if they will be regularly shaded and damp; red sandstone, for instance, may be beautiful but can be extremely hazardous, and in a damp climate will need a sterilizing wash every three months – hardly user friendly. Other sandstones with riven surfaces perform better and are available in many shades from cream to dark grey. Granite, slate and marble are expensive but wonderful pavers, though they must have roughened surfaces if used in a damp climate. The travertine marbles in particular look superb, though there is an attractive concrete substitute which can be used instead. Smooth, finely cut stone flags are better laid in a geometrical pattern, but consider the plan in Chapter 2 (page 28) which shows the principles for laying paving slabs in a random pattern which suits coarser stone and is both practical and attractive. Otherwise, consolidated gravel can be pleasantly crunchy to walk on and, if laid properly, is free draining.

The photograph on page 102 shows a garden where a combination of gravel and paving has been used. Rolling, raking and careful use of an appropriate weedkiller is all the care that is needed. However, growing plants through gravel in a sunny garden can be both charming and practical. In this case, a layer of binding gravel must be rolled in below the 75–100mm (3–4in) layer of clean surface gravel. Alternatively, there are woven or pierced plastic sheetings available to lay below the shingle, through which slitted planting holes can be cut and surface water drained away. This is convenient for small spaces as it suppresses weeds, although it also inhibits random seed dispersal which can be a pity, and it can also cause the gravel to slide on the surface. Some small plants which grow successfully in gravel are listed on page 58.

TIMBER

Timber decking is one of the most welcoming types of practical flooring. It is warm and quiet underfoot and blends well with virtually all surrounding architectural styles. It should be properly constructed on

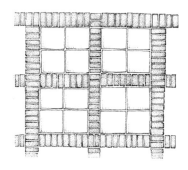

Fig 3 Formal and informal combinations of stone slabs and bricks.

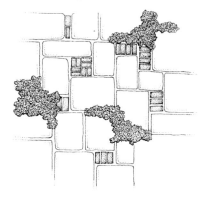

SMALL PLANTS FOR CREVICES IN PAVING

Acaena 'Blue Haze' or 'Copper Carpet'
Armeria caespitosa
Chamaemelum nobile 'Treneague'
Cotula lineariloba
Dianthus deltoides 'Bright Eyes'
Dianthus 'Little Jack'
Draba repens
Frankenia thymaefolia
Pratia pedunculata
Raoulia australis
Sagina subulata
Saxifraga 'Gaiety' (mossy)
Sisyrinchium bellum
Soleirolia soleirolii syn. *Helxine soleirolii*
Thymus doefleri
T. herba-barona
T. lanuginosus
T. serpyllum
Veronica prostrata 'Blue Sheen'

concrete footings with air circulating below, and only pressure-preservative treated timber or hardwood decay-resistant timbers should be used. Either allow the wood to age gracefully or use a wood stain. Draining water from the surface is important and if the site is in permanent dark shade which is usually damp, do not consider decking. Professional advice and construction is to be recommended.

Aesthetically, this is an attractive medium which is easy to care for, and laying the boards creates design opportunities. Parallels, either length or widthways, create neat rectangular forms, while the unexpected diagonal introduces a dynamic into the design. Timber decking looks good with pools, particularly when slightly overhanging and creating dark shadows below.

Reusing old railway sleepers can be an attractive alternative. These are totally weatherproof and durable, but do realize that both Douglas fir and Keruning, from which they are made, exude sticky tar-like substances which, when mixed with creosote, can be pretty messy. Take care to ensure that this will not continually ooze out as, once on the soles of shoes, it can cause real problems. Using sleepers as retaining walls for raised planting or for terracing, both vertically and horizontally, is nevertheless an attractive and effective proposition.

Grass

However tiny the plot, some people do want a green sward. In the photograph on page 137, a beautifully maintained minute lawn is a major feature and vital to this stylish garden, but it is caringly cultivated and lavished with affection. Generally, in the user-friendly small garden I would suggest that lawns are to be avoided. They need a great deal of care and cutting equipment must be stowed. Green substitutes like Chamomile 'Treneague'; Korean grass (*Zoysia tenuifolia*) for warm climates; helxine (*Soleirolia soleirolii*), for shade in mild areas; Corsican mint (*Mentha requienii*) and creeping thymes will all provide very flat green surfaces. Some, like the chamomile and thyme, can be walked upon, but they are not substitutes for functional lawns. What they add is easy, care-free and flat spaces which are visually tranquil, green and not onerous for the owner.

Contrasts

Mixed paving can often be an answer to the small site. Bricks can be used to edge formal, geometrically laid slabs or, to create a more informal look, reused frost-resistant bricks blend well with randomly placed paving and inset 'mat' planting like the thymes and chamomile (Fig 3 opposite). Granite setts perform just as successfully if brick does not suit the house. Then again, adding tiles with stone or fitting tiles into exposed aggregate concrete is another successful mix. Concrete looks better when edged, and brick, tiles, granite, cobbles or treated timber can all be used for this. As expansion joints are necessary anyway, tiles or other materials can do the job for you and also be decorative (Fig 4).

Fig 4 An exposed aggregate concrete path can be enhanced with different edgings and expansion joints.

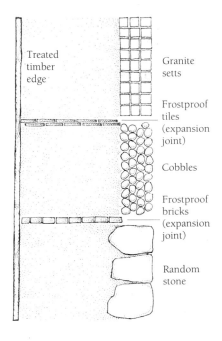

Treated timber edge

Granite setts

Frostproof tiles (expansion joint)

Cobbles

Frostproof bricks (expansion joint)

Random stone

However, when mixing hard materials in this way, it is important to realize that if you have a contrast of textures, you should avoid a contrast of colour as well: for example, pale sandstone slabs edged with red brick, quite a common combination, can be restive and jarring. Contrast must be kept in check. In just the same way, fluorescent white cottages in green countryside stand out too much; in the past, the original 'white wash' quickly became greyed and the houses merged with the countryside. As an alternative, pastel earth colours are more sympathetic. Equally clumsy, in my view, is the strong black-painted emphasis given to Tudor houses in England where the structural timbers contrast darkly with brilliant white paint. How much nicer the houses look when the timber is a mellow, aged grey. The textural contrast of the materials is still there, but it is far more subtle.

This should be borne in mind when using contrasting paving materials: if there is a colour contrast then textural contrast should be reduced, and vice versa.

Generally speaking, contrast always needs careful handling, particularly in the small garden where it must be considered within the overall design. This is a busy, small area with a lot happening and simplicity is the key. You need to balance the area of hard landscape with the areas of green; as with the Tudor houses, if the two areas are equally eyecatching the result is one of unease. It is far better to make one more dominating that the other, so that the onlooker does not have to make an agitated selection. It does not matter whether it is the paved or the green area which dominates, but one should be considerably more important than the other.

The small garden can have very little paving but be awash with plants and beautiful, as in the plant collectors' gardens in Chapter 6. Or it could be dominated by paving, with very subordinate planting, as in the mirror garden in Chapter 2. Balance is so important to good design.

SOILS

A word about soils is relevant here. As we are concerned with the easy-care nature of the garden it is important to work the soil well and provide for healthy, robust plants. Having established what type of soil you have – whether it is acidic or alkaline (use a soil-test kit), and whether it is heavy clay or sandy and insubstantial – you should be sure to condition it physically, as well as incorporate good 'slow-release' fertilizers. Good cultivation always pays off. Once your shrubs are established you are unlikely to be able to get under the roots again, so preparing thoroughly is really a 'one-off' and you won't have to repeat it. Peat and rotted, chopped bark or other fibrous and composted materials, with either coarse sand or grit, and deep digging can greatly improve the drainage and health of heavy soils. Sandy soils are often poor nutritionally, as well as draining very quickly, so adding bulky manures will help.

PLANTS FOR GROWING IN GRAVEL

Sh=Shrub
H=Herbaceous perennial

Basic
Small shrubs
Grasses
Very dwarf conifers

Smaller shrubs and perennials
Achillea (alpine) H
Alchemilla alpina H
Bulbs: *allium, crocus, eranthis, iris, narcissus, tulipa* ssp.
Campanula (alpine) H
Convolvulus cneorum Sh
Coronilla Sh
Diascia Sh
Euphorbia (dwarf) H
Festuca
Geranium (alpine) H
Hebe (dwarf) Sh
Hosta (small) H
Hypericum (dwarf) Sh
Hyssopus officinalis Sh
Ipheion uniflorum H
Iris (dwarf bearded vars) H
Lavandula (dwarf) Sh
Oreganum H
Phormium (small) Sh
Salvia officinalis vars Sh
Sedum vars H
Sisyrinchium H
Viola H

Larger shrubs and perennials
Acanthus spinosus H
Acer Sh
Artemisia H
Ballota pseudodictamnus Sh
Carpenteria californica Sh
Daphne Sh
Eremurus H
Eryngium H
Euphorbia characias H
E. mellifera H
Foeniculum vulgare H
Iris H
Phormium Sh
Potentilla H
Sarcococca confusa Sh
Verbascum H

Organic fertilizers like bonemeal, hoof and horn or fish, blood and bone are the traditional fertilizers. They release minerals over a period of time, thus reducing the need for frequent topping up. There are also extremely versatile synthesized fertilizers which are accurate and specific to multiple requirements. The needs of the soil and the intended plants will affect your selection, so advice from the manufacturers or garden centres should be sought. On the other hand, too much cossetting can kill – a quick 'shot in the arm' may help chlorosis (iron deficiency), but otherwise overfeeding *is* possible. This can reduce the efficiency of the plant system, causing weakened, forced growth and even death, so do resist the temptation to scatter fertilizers with casual largesse. If in doubt, leave alone rather than over-indulge.

WATERING

Watering is another concern about which there can be confusion. A quick top-up before going to work in the morning is not the answer. Roots seek water, and if that water is only in the very top of the soil they will come up for it and then, poor things, gasp, as the top soil dries out. Here again, if you can't be bothered or don't have time to do it properly, leave it alone and choose plants which will cope with all that you fail to throw at them.

Otherwise, when you do water, a fine spray for an hour will soak down to a good depth which will last for days, even in hot, dry weather. Particular care is necessary around the house and boundary walls. Many climbers struggle because the rain rarely penetrates within 12cm (5in) of the wall. Clematis in particular must drink, so try the method shown in Fig 5, which is easy and effective. Plastic tubing will take a can of water directly to the roots of the plant. Incidentally, as clematis are also very greedy, it is a good idea to add liquid fertilizer to the water once a fortnight.

There are irrigation systems available to replace manual duty. These can be controlled by timers and are the ultimate well-judged, easy-care system. Your only responsibility is to pay the water and electricity bills.

PLANTS

Now for the plants. How to plant with some style must, as with the hard landscaping, relate to the needs of the owner. I once had to design a smallish town garden where there were two rottweilers and a German shepherd dog. The 'rotties' were quite friendly but they saw no barriers to their exuberance. Where a smaller dog would go round they leapt over, rather inefficiently, and broke the growth of young shrubs; even the prickliest of plants failed to present a challenge. A garden full of specimen trees should have been the answer and I am sure would have delighted them, but it was a small place. All I can say is that I did my best.

Small children also threaten fragile foliage, but they are generally more amenable than dogs and can be gently advised to go round barriers. I

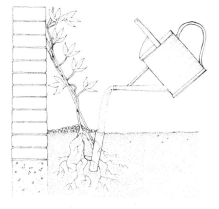

Fig 5 Clematis are easily fed and watered through plastic tubing.

have found that clipped box hedges act as clear 'no-go' areas to toddlers so that herbs and flowers can be grown within. The photograph above shows a town garden where a very large paved area provides space for trikes, bikes, and a moveable sand pit. Wide, shallow steps lead to the grass for further play, while box hedging clearly separates the herbs, irises and roses from the paving. In this case the affectionate labrador seems to recognize the barrier and, unless seduced by a badly aimed ball, does not trespass.

This garden was designed with the whole large family in mind. There is a big enough lawn with space for ball games; an old enough pear tree for a tree house; a smooth enough paved area for small wheels; and also sufficient space for adult pursuits. Box-edged beds border a seating area which accommodates a good number of people to dine outside. The beds allow for a variety of low shrubs and herbaceous plants and there are two overlapping boxed squares with a standard lollipop bay tree in the centre, around which grow culinary herbs. A wide-spreading cherry tree, *Prunus*

A big terrace provides space for large gatherings and for tricycles, sandpits and toys. A border of box hedging suggests a physical barrier to young children and the family dog.

'Hokusai', was planted to provide shade, but died in a drought and is to be replaced. A very wide metal arch carries scented climbers above one of the seats and continues over the side steps, so helping to enclose the space. This is developing into a pretty garden which is also easily managed.

HEDGING

Other hedging, apart from box, can divide space and be simple to maintain. Yew hedging is to my mind the best and is not as slow as is often thought. It requires clipping only once a year. The red fruits are attractive but contain poisonous seeds, so yew is not suitable for a garden where young children play. Other conifers like *Thuja plicata* varieties provide dense green hedges which need clipping once a year, but most are more suited to boundaries as they tend to be tall and are fast growing. Hollies, hornbeam and beech can provide domestic-sized hedges requiring little cutting, but privet (*Ligustrum ovalifolium*), though so reliable, does have to be trimmed frequently, as does *Lonicera nitida*. Some hedges, like *Berberis stenophylla* and *Escallonia macrantha,* provide flowers and are still quite neat in habit, but others, like cultivars of *Rosa rugosa*, though pretty with continuous flowers, hips and yellow autumn colour, are casual in habit and, though very easy-care, suit an informal style of garden.

EVERGREENS

Evergreens provide the 'bones' of a garden and, in the context of easy living, they are invaluable. Conifers offer enormous variety of shape, colour and texture. Do bear in mind that many are programmed to become huge forest trees and that others, described as dwarf, are in reality slow growing, and may surprise you with their aspirations. Some shrubs, particularly pyracanthas, can and should be clipped occasionally to form neat patterns against a wall. Large-leaved invaluable friends like the laurel (*Prunus laurocerasus* forms) offer shiny foliage. The Portuguese laurel (*Prunus lusitanica*) provides an easy, dark background foil for other plants, and that most versatile yet taken-for-granted plant *Aucuba japonica* offers great variety of shiny foliage, spotted and dotted foliage, and also splashed and blotched foliage, which you may leave for a year but will return to find serene and healthy. There are other good evergreen sources like mahonias, viburnums, hollies, rhododendrons and skimmias. Many offer flowers at unusual times plus fruits, scents and variegated foliage. They are worth looking into.

Some smaller evergreen, grow-anywhere plants are worth knowing. *Euonymus fortunei* varieties will grow in shade and provide small variegated foliage. In sun, some of the smaller grey-leaved shrubs like santolina and lavender are useful and attractive, though they must be clipped early in the year, after the last frost and then again after flowering. Then there are the wide-spreading conifers like *Juniperus sabina* var. *tamariscifolia*, varieties of *Juniperus procumbens* in golden or blueish hues, creeping yew (*Taxus baccata* 'Repandans'), dramatic *Picea pungens* 'Prostrata' and *Pinus mugo* var. *pumilio,* which have very different visual appeal. However, 'wide-spreading' can mean 3m (10ft) or more, so take care.

GROUND COVER

Ground covers are also apt to be territorially ambitious. They include small vincas, lamium, bugle, cinquefoil, cerastium, ivies and others at the lowest level. Slightly more variety can be achieved with grass-like foliage from liriope, festuca, ophiopogon, *Luzula sylvatica*, day lilies, hypericum and ferns.

CASE STUDY

A Garden for Containers

A completely different way of tackling the easy-care garden is to create a strong foundation of shrubs and climbers and add to it seasonally.

The garden plan opposite shows a garden which does this. It is extremely narrow and set at an awkward angle to the house. The layout aimed to distract attention from these faults, and for the same reason a false level was introduced by adding a 10cm (4in) high step. As seen in the photograph opposite, gravel is the main medium, with paving and brick edging adding variety. Along the walls the planting is very simple and the beds very small. A focal arbour made of metal effectively screens the utilitarian shed and can be seen in the photograph below.

A small arbour at the far end of the garden provides a focus as well as helping to conceal the functional garden shed.

Right: Diagonally-planned spaces add an illusion of width.

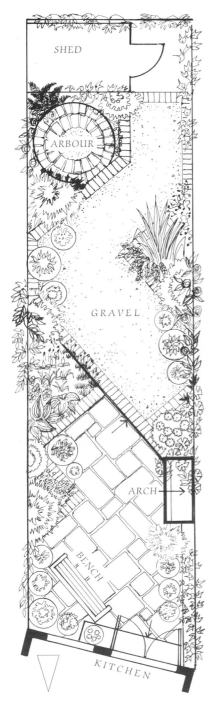

A Garden for Containers
The garden was planned to overcome problems of narrowness and the awkward angle of the house.

The owners laid out the garden themselves. What makes this a most charming and personal garden is the use of annuals and summer bedding plants. A good eye for colour plus dutiful watering and feeding has maintained luscious, flowing flowers. Different containers with highly attractive planting schemes fill the garden with brilliant colours in the sun. Culinary herbs have been treated in the same way, for as well as being useful, they can be very charming. This garden, once made, has proved to be easily managed. The owner has a very full professional life but derives great pleasure from the creative combinations of annuals and she can change the compositions each year. Watering is the main obligation, but the containers are small and this is quickly achieved each evening. In spring, bulbs fill the same pots and are then transplanted out. Even in winter there are winter pansies, which can be supported with ivies of all patterns and shapes.

Steps down to a basement can be gloomy, but container planting which can be moved around easily livens the whole scene.

The basement steps in the photograph above also show how the right selection of 'temporary' plants can brighten the darkest and plainest areas. Busy lizzies, pelargoniums, petunias and pink verbenas make these very utilitarian steps charming and friendly, and yet the effect was quite simple to achieve.

CASE STUDY
A Sunken Roof Garden

This sunken rooftop garden, protected from the wind, provides plenty of space for communal use. Interesting ceramic sculptures and furniture provide year-round charm.

Altogether different is the roof garden shown below. This is no DIY garden, but a carefully designed and constructed scheme for multiple use by surrounding apartments. Particular considerations apply to roof gardens. Structures should be lightweight, drainage particularly accurately handled, and both materials and plants should be carefully selected, being subject to extremes of weather: heat becomes focused on still days by surrounding buildings, and the cold is also that much more extreme. But it is wind which can be the most daunting problem. Here, some of these constraints have been avoided by sinking the garden below roof level – an interesting contradiction in terms; thus over-exposure, which can be the death of roof gardens, has been avoided.

This garden was designed by Victor Shanley for a very central site in London. It is subject to heavy use, but little time is available for maintaining the garden in detail. Consequently, there is foundation planting in raised beds consisting of flowering evergreen shrubs like pieris, skimmia, cistus and viburnum. Variegated leaves add lightness in winter and the stylish *Aralia elata* 'Variegata' (Japanese angelica tree), provides dappled shade under the canopy of its huge bi-pinnate leaves.

This also flowers: in late summer large fluffy panicles of cream flowers develop around the central axis of the stem. As with the container garden on page 64, annuals such as pelargoniums add colour. There are also evergreen climbers like ivies and flowering ones such as wisteria, roses and solanum.

Much has been made of the structural features. Victor used stainless-steel yacht fittings as taut parallel wire boundaries around the courtyard, and these attractive modern fittings blend superbly with the image of the garden. Timber trellis made from vertical slats also encourages the feeling of enclosure. The originality of the garden design is furthered by beautifully designed ceramic furniture which is like free-standing sculpture but with a lighthearted touch – take a look at the blue ceramic fat cat. Further fun can be seen in the ceramic 'cushions', which have the same duality of purpose. The benches were designed in Denmark by Hans and Birgitte Borieson and the cushions by Betty Engholm.

There are actually two of these sunken roof gardens with a passage between them. They serve the people who live in the penthouses and demonstrate ideas and a planting style which are extremely simple to maintain. This is truly a user-friendly garden, but with a style all its own.

Humour is always welcome in a garden. Ceramic 'cushions' may be sat upon and the blue ceramic cat is always there to be stroked.

5·Food for Thought

'…the serious intention of growing a great variety of food and herbs can be so very pleasantly linked with the pleasures of growing plants beside them for purely ornamental reasons.'

Evidence of growing food within a garden goes back to ancient times. Often relatively small in scale, these gardens of the past were concerned mainly with provision for the palace, castle, manor or monastery within whose walls they were contained. This was not farming in the sense of the corn belts of the USA, but intimate smallholdings of self-sufficiency which provided fruit, herbs and vegetables for a limited number of people. The gardens were mostly inward looking, being surrounded by walls, cloisters, hedges or trellis; they were probably labour intensive and, being functional, nearly always planned with convenient access, that is with limited size of planting beds and many paths.

A LITTLE HISTORY

Such gardens fed the body, but they also nurtured the spirit. Even the gardens of Egypt and Rome were planned to enhance life. The care devoted to the style of the garden and the use of decorative plants like roses and lilies show how deeply these gardens were valued. Skill in horticulture and an increasing knowledge of plant potential developed alongside the gardens and was passed on to successive generations. In many cases plants were trained over arbours or pergolas for practical purposes, but also to create areas of shade. Trees with wide canopies were chosen for the same reason. Essential water was supplied as small channels and pools, and these eventually became inspirational. Water could be used not only to support plants and to farm fish, but also to provide charming and playful rills and fountains, all to be incorporated within these small gardens.

As so much was expected of confined spaces and the gardens were pretty labour intensive, the layout had to be practical and efficient to run, so the spaces were split into workable units. Systems were devised for sectioning a rectangular garden space into the increasingly complicated patterns of the French 'potager' where vegetables, herbs and flowers could be grown, and in Europe these gradually evolved into the entirely decorative, almost plantless, 'knot' and 'parterre' gardens. Small hedging created patterns which were initially simple, being practical divisions of a planting area, but these too eventually developed into fantasized, extravagant elaboration. Sometimes they contained coloured gravels and sands, often excluding plants altogether, but the original ideas lived on and are popular again today.

Monastic gardens, though essentially sources of food and medicines, were also places of meditation, in which the senses were stirred. Taste, smell and sight were part of the total experience of the medieval garden. Later, more flowers and shrubs were added, as were features like arbours, seats, trellis and fountains. The layouts were quartered, then divided again. Shapes overlapped shapes, enclosing yet more detailed planting compartments. Peripheral wide paths coped with wheeled containers or carts, and very small paths, woven into the design, provided sufficient access to care for the plants.

'Pleasaunce' gardens of wild-flower meadows and fruit trees were forerunners of the 'hort-yard'. Gradually these became more varied, as the crusaders returned from Arab lands with descriptions of wonderful gardens. The more exotic trees like citrus and date palms would not survive in cooler climates, but apple, cherry, chestnut, pear, plum, quince and medlar grew productively alongside indigenous ash, beech, hazel, holly, holm oak, maple, yew, cypress and pine, becoming the subjects of carefully planned orchards.

In the meantime, the peasant too had to provide for a family. This would originally have fulfilled a serious life or death function, but in England by Victorian times it had become romanticized as the cottage garden, portrayed in whimsical paintings showing leisurely maintenance of flower gardens, where the hollyhocks and poppies were more evident than the cabbages and carrots.

However, we are now a privileged generation and, by buying time, we are returning once again to the enormous pleasure of growing our own, 'organic' food in allotments and also in gardens. It is rather reassuring to find that we can make gardens with exactly the same aims as those of so long ago: that the serious intention of growing a great variety of food and herbs can be so very pleasantly linked with the pleasures of growing plants beside them for purely ornamental reasons. The picture opposite shows a mix of herbs – thymes, sage and mint – happily allied with poppies, French lavender and santolina.

LAYOUT

If you aim to create a 'potager' or 'parterre' style of garden in your small plot, it is important to consider first the style and then the shapes you require. With this come decisions on the planning of the pathways which will provide access. No matter if your plot is not geometrically bounded: awkward spaces are easily filled with shrubs. Clear delineation suits the ornamental kitchen garden, making it much easier to manage and providing an attractive layout. The total space and its subdivisions are usually best handled with the simplest geometry; elaborately shaped beds will conflict with the rich tapestry of plant shapes in summer and make for confused design.

This attractive herb garden gives an indication of the variety of shapes, textures and colours that herbs provide.

Small Gardens with Style

Fig 1 These boxed gardens are on very different scales. The first one is very small indeed compared with the third one, which may well take up the whole of a small garden. The fourth plan suggests a combination of hedges with setts as edges for this circular design.

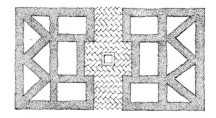

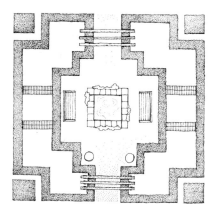

Fig 1 suggests some simple approaches to creating formal beds. These show plans on different scales, and are intended as some initial thoughts which you may develop in your own way.

Do bear in mind that box and other hedges will need clipping but are tidy, whereas other soft edging may be easier and cheaper but less neat. The style you choose must suit the time you have to spend in the garden. Alternative edging like tiles, setts, timber slats or bricks may suit you rather better.

When such geometric patterns were originally made they were simple, and included many medicinal and some culinary herbs. There were also some vegetables and fruit and a changing supply of annual and perennial flowers. Adding arches and pergolas, elaborate spires of trellis or pyramids of stakes, all creating sculptural forms at regular intervals within the design, made for a 'potager' effect which has become fashionable again. If climbers require supporting structures these could be as decorative as in any other part of the garden, and recently ready-made frames as 'obelisks' of wood or metal have become commercially available for the vegetable plot. The DIY answer to this is to make tall, slender 'wigwams' of canes or, better still, whippy hazel or wands of willow which can be bent to make less stiff alternative towers. Beans of all types, peas, loganberries and tayberries are the sorts of plants which will grow on them. You could also add colour; annual climbing nasturtiums, ipomoea or decorative gourds, grown from seed, are some ideas. If the obelisk is strongly made and you site a few of them in the garden you could introduce climbing roses, which are very decorative as well as acting as warning signals that mildew is around.

HEDGES AND EDGES

Often a combination of a 'parterre' garden and a French 'potager' garden is what is required. Parterres were traditionally edged with box (*Buxus sempervirens*), but equally effective as clipped dwarf hedges were Old English Lavender (*Lavandula spica*), cotton lavender (*Santolina chamaecyparissus*), or wall germander (*Teucrium fruticans*). You could consider using any of these today. However, there are other alternatives for more informal edging to outline the beds. In this case thymes (*Thymus serpyllum*), thrift (*Armeria maritima*), chives (*Allium schoenoprasum*), dwarf pinks like the clove pink (*Dianthus caryophyllus*), *Dianthus deltoides* varieties, the smaller hardy geraniums like *G. subcaulescens*, or *G. sangineum*, or the mossy saxifrages are all very low-level edgers. Slightly larger edging plants are also useful. The smaller varieties of day lilies, *Liriope muscari* and mondo grass (*Ophiopogon japonicus*) provide grassy edgings. *Stachys lanata* and the gently coloured grey, purple and yellow sages provide soft, almost velvet edgings, while the invaluable *Alchemilla mollis* and the hardy geranium family offer many slightly taller alternatives, of which *Geranium renardii*, *G. sylvaticum* 'Album' and *G.* 'Johnson's Blue' are representative.

PATHS

Paths are functional but also decorative features within the potager. They should be comfortably wide to allow for some overlap of plant material. Ideally, the width would also cope with a wheel-barrow: 1 – 1.5m (3 – 5ft) is perfect. However, in very small plots it is still possible to include a path only 60 – 80cm (2 – 2 ½ft) wide.

Paths can be paved with a variety of materials. Gravel can be used but it should be hard-rolled, properly cambered, and the surface would be better if only 6 –10mm (¼ – ½in) graded sharp gravel or shingle were used. The advantages of gravel are that it is inexpensive, adapts well to curves and offers a choice of soft colours to blend with local building materials. Set against this, remember that gravel is apt to travel and can also present difficulties in the fall when leaves may need picking up by hand. An edge restraint of either treated timber, purpose-made tiles or brick on edge will also be necessary.

Brick paths always look good in the kitchen garden. They must be frostproof or specially suited brick pavers. The choices of pattern between 'herringbone', 'basketweave' or 'running bonds' (see page 34) will depend upon the layout of the beds. Diagonal lines can be met easily with herringbone or running patterns but, interestingly, herringbone also suits rectangular paths when laid at 90°. This is more costly than laying it at 45°, as it means cutting the bricks at the edges unless the path is not to be restrained, in which case the zig-zag edging can be very attractive.

If you do not choose gravel, curved paths can be extremely attractive using squared granite setts or smooth, flattish cobbles. As these are smaller-sized units they can follow curves much more easily than bricks. All of these materials should be laid with a cross-fall to drain surface water into the beds. Some people like rotted, chopped bark for paths, but amongst vegetables this covering can harbour undesirables like slugs, and as birds root for them much of your expensive bark ends up on the beds.

BOUNDARIES

Larger, denser perimeter hedging may be needed to frame your ornamental kitchen garden. Few of us have high brick-wall boundaries. Hedging is protective but does allow some air to penetrate, and this discourages cold air from being trapped at ground level, creating frost pockets.

Traditional hedges of conifers like yew (*Taxus baccata*), *Thuja plicata* and Leyland cypress are evergreen, but beech retains attractive leaf cover in winter, albeit dead, and hornbeam is nearly as effective. Informal hedging like *Rosa rugosa*, fuchsia, escallonia, cotoneaster and berberis can add the charms of flower, scent and fruit. Old ideas of creating fences from willow or hazel woven into windbreak palisades, known as wattle, can be explored, or the very ancient but effective living fence where fresh stakes of hawthorn, willow and briar rose are planted firmly together in parallel. Most of them will root to form a mixed-thicket, thorny hedge.

Painted timber

Metal

Trellis

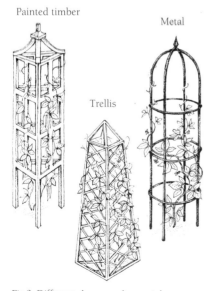

Fig 2 Different shapes and materials are suggested for obelisks which will support plants like runner beans, sweet peas or even decorative gourds.

One result which must be borne in mind when planting any living barrier is what goes on underground. The roots will compete with your plants for water and for food, so add fertilizer to your hedges and do not plant other things too close to them.

Sometimes trained fruit trees can be used to mark boundaries along paths. Indeed, the careful pruning of many fruit trees increases cropping. They can be shaped on walls or as free-standing hedges, their regular forms creating decorative linear patterns. Free-standing trees depend upon horizontally parallel, taut wires to support the shape, and most will look better on walls, where the reflected warmth helps to ripen the fruit. The 'espaliered' pattern, however, adapts well, to provide a boundary between planting bed and path.

FOCAL POINTS

A further consideration when laying out an ornamental vegetable garden is that despite strong structure and the emphasis of paths, the garden will become a beautiful but confusing tangle of overlapping shapes and colours by the height of summer. It is therefore a good idea to provide a permanent focus, a place for the eye to rest, which need not be central but must be dominating.

A well-sited seat or arbour provides just such a stopping place and is also an inducement to participate in the garden. Rose bowers, trellised arches or simply seats enclosed in flowery hedging can be eyecatchingly beautiful. Most designs work better with a 'full stop' to which the eye is led, otherwise the whole garden becomes so much endlessly decorative wallpaper. Traditionally, a sculpture, a well, an arbour or a fountain would have been included, and one of these could be adapted to suit the scale of your site or the size of your purse. Alternatively, one striking small tree such as the grey-leaved weeping pear (*Pyrus salicifolia* 'Pendula') or *Fagus sylvatica* 'Purple Fountain' would do just as well. Amongst conifers, *Juniperus virginiana* 'Skyrocket' has the narrowest dimension, but I prefer the Irish *J. communis* 'Hibernica', which has a far denser texture though it is also wider. Both are blue-green, particularly 'Skyrocket', and aim at a height of 5 – 6m (16 – 19ft). As they are rather slim, one on its own would look forlorn; a group of three would have more impact.

Other dramatic profiles can be 'carved' from box, yew or holly. Topiary has a place here. Tall, narrow forms, rounded domes, elongated pyramids or quite elaborate tiered shapes can be created. If you have the skill, you may have a fancy for an heraldic mythical bird or beast, or then again, perhaps a portrait of the cat — each to their own. (One very charming garden which I know has rows of giant heads, all female, all grotesques. I guess the owner has something to work out.) Then again you could consider clipped 'lollipops' of bay, or marguerites or roses fountaining from a single stem, all of which will provide a focus. Half-standard gooseberry bushes are also very pretty. So, as you can see, it does not have to be only hard materials which provide such features.

Fig 3 Training fruit trees.

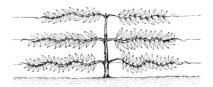

Espalier

Cordon

Fan

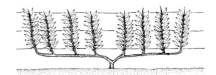

Vertical cordon

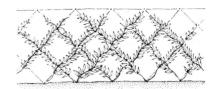

Large-scale lattice

Evening sunlight reveals the rich patterns and shapes of this ornamental kitchen garden.

The photograph above shows a very beautiful ornamental kitchen garden with a most unusual central polyhedron sculpture. This is made from an inverted pyramid set within another pyramid. Being centrally sited, the sculpture dominates the planting of the beds, which contain chives as edging plants, blue flowers of the Chinese forget-me-not (*Cynoglossum boraginacea*), with alliums, lettuces and four half-standard gooseberry bushes.

The most common focal point, that of a sundial, can be seen in the very pretty herb garden pictured on page 69. Here it is sited in a traditionally central position, open to the sun and surrounded by French lavender, santolina, thymes, sages, mint and self-seeding poppies.

FOOD AND ORNAMENT IN THE KITCHEN GARDEN

The serious business of growing food does not exclude possibilities for visual charms as well. It goes without saying, of course, that kitchen gardens should primarily be concerned with flavour as well as 'taste'. Here, however, I shall concentrate on visual aesthetics as an extra dimension when choosing vegetables, fruit or salads.

Basic decisions must be made first. How much space is to be allocated to root and leaf? That is, how much to carrots and parsnip, or celeriac and kohlrabi, compared with calabrese and cabbage, or broccoli and Swiss chard? You will probably wish to grow salad vegetables like lettuces, endive and rocket, plus the 'fruits' – tomatoes, peppers, aubergines and so on – and these can be very decorative plants. New varieties are produced regularly, and many are visually pretty or unusual. Yellow tomatoes like 'Golden Perfection', or striped ones like 'Tigerella' are a surprise.

Some of the seed and pod vegetables offer more visual alternatives. Runner beans have different flower colours, from red and orange to a bi-coloured red-and-white flower called 'Painted Lady'. There is also a white one named 'Polestar'. Then there are yellow-podded beans called 'Goldperle' and 'Mont d'Or', which not only add colour but are exceptionally good to eat. Okra too has a pretty flower, and asparagus peas have garnet-red flowers as well as very attractive wing-like pods. Peas, too, offer coloured pods of yellow and purple, while bulb vegetables like onions can have charming flowers, as many of the allium family testify. The photograph below shows some magnificent maize with blue seakale (*Crambe maritima*), and vivid scarlet runner beans. The foliage of leeks creates other linear, rhythmic patterns of bluish-green, adding variety to the plot. Further interest could be provided by the distinguished shapes found amongst the squash group, some of which have extraordinary form. The skin colours can be yellow or green, or

This photograph shows the great decorative value given by a potager in late summer.

have patterned surfaces like those on courgettes and marrows. You may also like to try growing annual ornamental (non-edible) gourds just for fun.

The flowers of the courgette *are* edible, which leads me to suggest that other flowers can be grown for eating, like nasturtiums, pot marigold, blue borage flowers and of course rose petals. However, always be sure to check: poisonous plants can have seductively beautiful flowers, like those of aconites or belladonna, and should never be associated with edible garden plants.

In your kitchen garden you may choose to grow only permanent easy-to-care-for plants if time is short. Some of these can be very stylish. Cardoon and asparagus add visual contrast, rhubarb needs little care and ruby chard is an extremely striking red. Then, you could include some decorative plants: honesty (*Lunaria annua*), for example, which is biennial and seeds promiscuously everywhere, would add purple, white, or a mixture of both, early in the year and particularly striking paper-white seed pods in winter. Consider also how well some of the late chrysanthemums (now renamed) such as *Dendranthema* 'Anastasia' will look. There are 'old bronze' colours, dusky pinks and lemon yellows, all of which will brighten the ornamental kitchen garden as autumn closes in.

HERBS

Herbs have become an obsession with some people, and it is often forgotten how very untidy and greedy for space many of them can be as they are attractive, often scented and have nostalgic associations. You can use them successfully on their own, though, making a formal herb garden within a boxed plan. Be sure to keep the more rampant mints planted in containers to control their prowess.

Culinary herbs are usually softly coloured, the brightest being golden marjoram. There is a yellow-leaved sage, *Salvia officinalis* 'Icterina', but the usual cooking sage is grey. Rosemary has blue flowers, and there can be no bluer leaf than that of rue (*Ruta graveolens*). A rich brown colour is found in bronze fennel (*Foeniculum vulgare*), and the range of greens covers everything from bright emerald parsley to soft grey-green salad burnet.

Herbs are strikingly variable in size, habit and texture. Some lend themselves to neat formality, fitting snugly into small spaces; amongst these are small thymes, marjoram, parsley and chives. Others can be of tree-like proportions, the largest being bay, though rosemary and *Angelica archangelica* can reach over 2m (7ft). Bay can of course be grown as a sculpted pyramid or as a single-stemmed clipped lollipop. Fennel, too, is tall, usually reaching 1.5m (5ft). In between heights of 30 – 90cm (1 – 3ft) are more usual: mints, sage, basil, chervil, coriander, dill and sorrel are amongst those which fall into this group. Textures also vary, from finely feathery like fennel and chervil (*Anthriscus cerefolium*), to prettily lacy, like sweet cicely (*Myrrhis odorata*) and caraway (*Carum carvi*), tightly curled like parsley, or touchingly velvet like sage and woolly thyme. Visually, herbs are a treat, offering nearly as much variety of form and texture as herbaceous plants. But their charm is subtle rather than audacious, which is why they have such appeal.

Medicinal herbs, whether accurately attributable or not, are just as varied in form, colour and habit. Some may be poisonous like monkshood (*Aconitum napellus*), and foxglove (*Digitalis purpurea*), or be much favoured by herbalists, like evening primrose (*Oenothera biennis*), or feverfew (*Chrysanthemum parthenium*). But they are also very pretty – those mentioned above have deep blue, purple, yellow or white flowers respectively. There are very many others, and you may be interested in looking into the possibilities.

If you intend to retain a section of your small garden for herbs only, do bear in mind that this is yet another area in which you will have to make choices. As we have seen, the heights of the plants vary enormously, so you will need space to show them at their best.

Herbs can be filtered into vegetable and flowerbeds quite informally. On the other hand, some will self-seed at an amazing rate, such as feverfew, lady's mantle (*Alchemilla mollis*), heartsease (*Viola tricolor*) and the mulleins (*Verbascum thapsus*). These will add unpredictable   patterns to those of your own devising; often lovely, but if not, they can be weeded out easily. The really strongly scented herbs like thyme, lemon balm, rosemary and lemon verbena should be planted near seats or close to the house so as not to miss out on their offerings.

The gentle foliage of the sages, whether grey, yellow or purple, blends with all plants in the sun. Some sages will not survive very low temperatures but are still worth growing, like pineapple sage, with its red flower and deliciously scented leaves. Other less hardy plants like parsley and French tarragon must be planted out annually; but a substantial design framework can be offered by forms of artemisia and santolina, by hyssop, golden marjoram, catmint, rue, alliums and chives.

As I have described, herbs come in many shapes and sizes and are used for culinary or medicinal purposes, but also, to be honest, they are often planted nowadays for their romantic associations as well.

FLOWERS WITH VEGETABLES AND HERBS

As the aim of both the herb garden and kitchen garden is to be always attractive as well as functional, annual flowers as well as herbaceous perennials can be used to advantage. Amongst the lettuces, onions, courgettes, broad or runner beans, artichokes and asparagus, grow marguerites, lupins, larkspur, wallflowers, hollyhocks, pinks or yarrow, further enhanced by scattered seeds of old-fashioned annuals, those loved by children for their instant effect, such as poppies, stocks, candytuft, clarkia, flax, nasturtiums and love-in-a-mist, all adding remembered charm. In particular, nasturtiums and pot marigolds mix gloriously with alliums and chervil, as seen in the photograph opposite.

Opposite: Annual flowers distributed among ornamental vegetables create a richly coloured and textured effect.

Other flowers which look particularly beautiful are the old roses, which were planted amongst the profusion of vegetables and fruits in castle and monastery gardens. A good example is *Rosa mundi*, syn. *R. gallica versicolor*, which is a rose of romantic associations thought to have been named after the fair Rosamund, mistress of Henry II of England. Whether this is true or not, it is a very pretty red-and-white striped rose which will make a 1.2m (4ft) high hedge. The apothecary's rose also has historical associations, as it was used for medicinal purposes in France. Its real name is *Rosa gallica* var. *officinalis* and it is probably of very ancient stock; the showy hips are exceptionally attractive in the fall. As some of the old roses are mildew prone, it might be worth considering some of the newer modern shrub roses, many of which are bred for attractive habit, foliage, fragrance, fruit and disease resistance. They can be grown as standards or as informal hedging, or trained over arches and pergolas, and would look good within the decorative kitchen garden.

The potager shown in the plan on this page is laid out on a strictly geometric pattern. An axial brick path leads to a central arbour which supports the runner beans. All the other paths are gravelled. The beds are slightly raised and the rich, deep soil is retained by lengths of timber pegged at the corners. Opposite the same garden is seen late in the year in its glorious close-to-harvest chaos. Rampant growth of artichokes, onions and broad beans tangles with the colourful vitality of sweet peas, nasturtiums and red ruby chard. These two pictures tell a story. Potager gardens, like herb gardens, start the year within their geometric bounds but as the seasons progress the plants become unruly children, taking advantage by spreading and overwhelming others with their sheer vitality. This is beautiful, but does require knowledgeable planting in the first place and informed care in the second. This charming, overflowing scene is under the relaxed control of its sensitive and experienced owners.

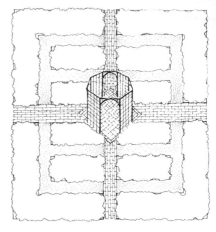

Fig 4 A plan of the potager pictured opposite. A simple layout allows easy access to rich planting.

Opposite: Looking towards the central arch where all paths meet, the frame supports annual sweet peas which add vitality to the artichokes, beets and onions.

UNUSUAL AND ATTRACTIVE VEGETABLES

Artichoke
Asparagus
'Mary Washington'
Aubergine
'Black Prince'
Bean, Runner
'Painted Lady' (red-and-white flowers)
'Pickwick' (orange flowers, dwarf)
'Polestar' (white flowers)
Bean, French
'Goldperle'
'Purple Podded'
Beetroot
'Red Ace'
'Forono'
Broccoli
'Romanesco'

'Red Arrow'
'Mercedes'
'Early Purple Sprouting'
Cabbage
'Ruby Ball'
'Red Dutch'
'January King'
Cape Gooseberry (Physalis edulis)
Capsicum (pepper)
'Midnight Beauty' (purple)
Cauliflower
'Snowcrown'
'Violet Queen'
Celery
'Giant Pink'
Chard
Ruby chard
Courgette
'Golden Zucchini'
Endive
'Ione'

Globe artichoke
'Green Globe'
Kale
'Dwarf Green Curled'
Leeks
'Walton Mammoth'
Lettuce
'Sangria'
'Lollo Rosso'
'Carnival'
'Red Salad Bowl'
Marrow
'Tivoli'
'Gold Rush'
'Zebra Cross'
Melon
'Ogen'
Okra
'Long Green'
'Clemson Spineless'
Onion
'Ishikura'

'North Holland Blood Red – Redmane'
Ornamental gourds
Pak choi
Pea
'Asparagus Pea'
'Oregon Sugar Pod'
Purslane
'Winter'
Radiccio
'Palla Rossa Bella'
Seakale beet
Squash
'Sweet Dumpling'
Sweet corn
'Mexican'
'Strawberry'
'Sundance'
Tomato
'Cherry Belle'
'Tigerella'
'Golden Sunrise'

Above: At the start of the season this potager by Rosemary Verey at Barnsley House is laid out in a distinctive square.

Left: More geometry and more fun, this time with lettuces which swirl into a pattern of concentric circles.

In contrast, the potager opposite above was photographed early in the year and the formal layout is clearly visible. Both the lettuce and the onions are decorative within the structure of the bed. For a total commitment to purely ornamental planting however, the photograph opposite below shows lettuce planted with great aplomb. This is an amusing and highly effective scheme, using one type of vegetable but in two colour variations, red and green.

Nevertheless, just look at the photograph below, where the association between a herb plant and a herbaceous perennial is highly original and very beautiful. This photograph was taken in a garden in France designed by Mark Brown, and the hazy foliage of the green fennel blends wonderfully with the warm orange of the geum and *Hieracium aurantiacum*.

These are just some of the possibilities which can be explored when creating an ornamental kitchen garden, thus taking the original parterred monastic gardens, potagers and the traditional 'cottage gardens' a stage further in design. The varieties of shapes, forms, textures and colours are considerable, and many more plants are becoming available as horticulturalists and farmers press on.

The gentle colourings and textures make this one of the most beautiful plant associations. Hazy green fennel merges with *Geum* x *borisii* and *Hieracium aurantiacum*.

6 · The Inspired Collector

'There are people whose love of plants is the whole source and inspiration for their gardens – but their gardens are not merely living museums.'

The eminent American landscaper Thomas Church wrote an extremely influential book titled *Gardens are for People*. This is such a complete statement and so simply effective that it is, for me, a guideline from which I never deviate. However, I have now to say: well, not quite always, they're not.

The gardens in this chapter are 'gardens for plants'. There are people whose love of plants is the whole source and inspiration for their gardens – but their gardens are not merely living museums. If they were just collections of plants, then the garden would be laid out on a grid pattern with plants divided and catalogued, as in a botanic garden. But the people I am writing about have 'an eye'. That is, they respond to garden-making as artists, who see the intrinsic beauty of each plant they collect and are able to intensify this within the garden context. The acquired prizes, given or bought, are placed with knowledgeable care in the company which fulfils their horticultural needs. But in these small gardens the sites are also chosen with visual compatibility in mind as well.

Bringing together plants with individual virtues of form, colour and texture so that each plant benefits its neighbour, while at the same time masterminding the whole picture, is no mean skill. The more there is to use, the more difficult is the composition. The plant specialist does not want to leave out plants as ruthlessly as the fine artist can omit aesthetic irrelevancies. This could be a painful process for the plantsman-artist when the acquisition and the display are both of equal value – but they can do it. The plant lovers in this chapter have made wonderful gardens without relinquishing their plants. Their judgement when placing plants together is usually influenced by a passion, whether for colour, form or other visual effect, and, by being so clearly directed, the total impression is one which pleases. So, these gardens are for people after all.

CHOOSING PLANTS

Choosing plants is exciting for all gardeners. From the first seed packet of 'Kiddies' Mixture', the thrill of owning and growing captures the imagination, and there has never been so much choice as there is today. Plant hunters have been let loose again and hybridizers challenge themselves. The fascination of plants appeals to a great number of people, from flower arrangers to tissue culturalists. New forms and rare species are becoming available to growers and thence to the public, and there are endless possibilities for the discriminating garden-maker.

Nurseries selling 'unusual' plants have been prospering. As garden owners become more involved they begin to branch out. Once the structure and year-round seasonal fluctuations have been established, gardeners then become interested in the detail of their gardens, and find that they have likes and dislikes. This can lead to real specialization within the garden and membership of societies like the Alpine Garden Society, the Hardy Plant Society and, even more specific, the Hosta and Hemerocallis Society, Iris Society and so forth.

But for many garden owners the preferences are more casual: it is the look and style of the whole garden which dominates their thoughts. Even the owner of a specialist rose collection realizes that roses look more fetching with alchemilla, geraniums, irises or nepeta at their feet.

CASE STUDY

A Plantswoman's Small Lot

Taking this to an unconventional and highly creative extreme is the tiny garden made by the artist Sheila Jackson, whose courtyard can be seen on the following pages. Truly an inspired collector, Sheila has produced a beautiful and fascinating garden in an incredibly limited space. This is probably the smallest garden in the book, yet it must be one with the greatest variety of plants.

THE LAYOUT The owner describes the garden as being originally a tiny yard of 'cracked concrete and stamped earth in which builders had buried all the rubble from the conversion of the substantial old house'. As Sheila is an artist she has used her seeing eye as the creative source for the garden plan. She has kept to a very simple scheme, allowing just enough room for her to tend the plants but without any sophisticated hard landscaping. Quite clearly there is the priority of plants over people. Even one seat would be problematical, as there would be no space to rest your feet. But, as she says, 'colour and shape are part of my trade'. The small space overflows with foliage and flowers. Many plants use one another for support, and layering is fabricated by mounding structures one upon another, so that there are containers even at head height and above.

However, as with all aesthetic ventures, planning may be concealed but it is there. The evergreen backing for the garden as a whole is thoughtfully selected to provide soft greenness all year round; it is the growing architecture of the garden. Some shrubs with large leaves are challengingly bold for the intimacy of the small yard, but it is with such unpredictable choices that the owner's creative flair is displayed. This garden is immediately adjacent to a main railway terminus. There must be a dozen busy tracks starting only 5m (15ft) away from the house, and yet the trains do not intrude. After a few minutes spent in this richly planted environment they are forgotten. What an achievement.

Tall, old brick walls add protection and also provide surfaces for climbers and wall shrubs. The layout also includes some low brick-built retained planting beds which curve around a concreted space, leaving a circle. In this, planters and pots cascade with flower and foliage. At the back, against the railway line, four 2m (6ft) high terracotta chimneys, recycled from the roof, act as Mycenean pillars supporting lintels of massed, intertwined climbers. Between the columns are three small alcoves, lit by shafts of viridescent light which pierce the green canopy of interwoven plants. The climbers are quite undisciplined and have ventured towards cables beside the railway. Whether they double as lightning conductors remains to be seen. The line inspectors regularly check the herbage and remove all threatening plant life as necessary!

Some plants grow from a reconditioned bed of soil retained by the low brick wall, and here they can root away as necessary, but mostly they grow in the many containers, both orthodox and ingenious. On shelves made from old marble slabs, built up with bricks from dismantled storage heaters, plant pots stand cheek by jowl upon one another. At the base of these constructions the plants are cool rooted, while at top they are exposed to heat and sun. The right plant in the right place is the owner's forte, and that is why they all thrive. In this way Sheila has provided for large plants, small ones, acid-lovers, plants for shade, for sun, damp plants and dry plants. All are carefully succoured as individuals and the results are splendid and fascinating.

The garden is seen as a three-dimensional space, not simply two-dimensional where plants are grounded, but with a truly theatrical depth in which the tiered constructions and plant holders suspended from the walls play their part. Sheila acquired increasing numbers of plants in containers and crammed every available space with them. Some containers fitted well into the top of the chimney pots, some are banked together, and others are quite large enough for shrubs.

THE PLANTING The one virtue of the site is that it is very sunny and sheltered. Thus some risks have been taken, and plants which would not normally survive at this latitude prosper within the microclimate of the garden. It will be seen from the photographs and the plants named below that this fact, plus good husbandry, has made it possible for the plants to form some very unlikely but successful liaisons. Handled with such delicacy, these associations may be geographically illogical but are nevertheless very attractive.

All of this could, of course, result in a chaotic jumble, were it not for the creative control of the owner. Sometimes it is the use of contrasting foliage which holds it all together, sometimes a gentle, restrained colour link. In one area silvers and greys are vitalized by soft yellow and cream colours, while blue hostas sharpen the mix. *Euphorbia wulfenii* is a strongly formed lime green against which *Convolvulus cneorum* provides silver-silk leaves and white flowers. *Lychnis coronaria* 'Alba' and a potentilla add more white flowers, and *Festuca glauca* fronting *Lonicera nitida* 'Baggesen's Gold' and a small golden bay (*Laurus nobilis* 'Aurea') link through with blue and yellow. Beyond this group, *Coronilla valentina*

Purple-grey and silver foliage of *Rosa rubrifolia* and *Stachys byzantina* add a cool note to the pale yellows and creams of the achilleas and the hosta.

'Citrina', *Cytisus* x *praecox* and the tall silver-leaved *Cytisus battandieri* link upwards to the climbers. Of these, *Akebia quinata* adds fragrant red flowers, evergreen *Clematis cirrhosa balearica* provides creamy flowers in winter, and the tender Botany Bay tea tree (*Correa alba*) has tubular white flowers in late summer. The last three climbers come from the Far East, the Balearics and Australia, an indication of the wide selection of plants in this tiny space.

All the above thrive under the concentration of sunshine in that part of the garden. Elsewhere, slightly more protected from the sun, a *Clematis montana* and *Solanum jasminoides* 'Album' provide more white flowers, though the former has to be tamed. Here, too, room has been made for

Lonicera fragrantissima, Abeliophyllum distichum, Mahonia haematocarpa and *Correa backhousiana*. The first two provide winter flowers and fragrance. The second two come from Texas and Tasmania, so here again the origins of the plants mean that careful siting and protection is important. Varieties of hellebores thrive in pots, as do *Dicentra macrocapnos* and *Brachyglottis* 'Sunshine'.

A shadier bank of pots faces the French window, providing homes for hostas, daphnes and a white lacecap hydrangea, plus taller *Sarcococca humilis* and *Ilex* 'Blue Angel'. Then *Colletia paradoxa* from South Africa, *Cestrum parqui* from Chile, *Choisya ternata* from Mexico and *Hebe salicifolia* from New Zealand follow through. *Darmeria peltata*, syn. *Peltiphyllum peltata,* grows out of a plastic bowl which is kept filled to the brim with water, its large leaves acting as a balance amongst the masses. The foliage of selected grasses, ferns and hostas has the same calming effect.

The flowerbed is loved as much as the foliage. Over the years this raised bed has received rich quantities of humus, thus improving the nutrition and structure of the soil. All sorts of hellebores, astrantias, epimediums, campanulas, roses, fuchsias, *Smilacina polygonatum* and alcea grow successfully. None are neglected, and all are comforted with experienced care. Some annuals are added, such as selected strains of nicotianas and pelargoniums, for seasonal variation.

Above: Hostas and hydrangeas with simple but striking forms contrast with the more detailed patterns of pink astrantia and *Ophiopogon nigrescens.*

Opposite: Dark heuchera foliage foots rodgersia, helichrysum, euphorbia and wildly self-seeding balsam, while dark red phormium and berberis echo the colour. All the plants are in containers that can be moved around.

Shades of white rise in tiers from stacked containers. Dimorpotheca, pelargoniums, hydrangeas and hostas are combined to create this effect.

At floor level, the cracks in the concrete have provided a home for *helxine (Soleirolia soleirolii), Cymbalaria muralis* and *Campanula poscharskyana*, and any other plants which distribute their charms by seed dispersal.

Clearly, the main colour theme of whites, greens and yellows holds the plant masses together. This is a designer's collection. Sheila's many beautiful watercolour paintings, recently published in book form, show her sensitive awareness of growth patterns, form, texture and colour, and the photographs here demonstrate that the careful grouping of plants, where each flatters another while at the same time relating to the whole, is totally harmonious. With her aesthetic gift, Sheila moves the containers around as plants wax and wane. Some need a rest and others have more to give. Expertise has come through the years, but the inborn creative vision is inspired by the vast variety and beauty of plants now available to gardeners, even in such very small spaces.

CASE STUDY

Two Foliage Enthusiasts

A totally different type of collection can be seen in the next two gardens, where foliage is all.

A 'WOODLAND' GARDEN The small garden owned by Peter Partridge rises steeply from the house, and has not been terraced. Instead, there is a distinctly woodland feel to the garden and a path meanders up around magnificent forms of leaves. As with the last garden, the hard landscaping is minimal, but there is a paved 'glade' for seating. At present, a huge *Salix matsudana* 'Tortuosa' dominates the garden in its central position. It has provided dappled shade which creates planting possibilities, but this is a fast-growing, large tree for a small garden and its days are probably numbered.

Plant largesse does not inhibit the owner of this garden. A vast Chinese necklace poplar (*Populus lasiocarpa*) is also a fast-growing tree, but the foliage of large heart-shaped, red-veined leaves has proved irresistible. Huge leaves like those of *Tetrapanax papyriferus*, syn. *Fatsia papyrifera*, which is protected in this site and grows in rich, moist soil, are dramatic to see, though do be aware that this plant expands by suckers.

Rhododendron sinogrande and *Magnolia delavayi* are two shrubs with some of the largest leaves of any evergreens in a temperate climate, and they both appear in this garden. A competitor for this title, *Trachycarpus fortunei*, is hardier and will not need the same care. The photograph of *Bergenia ciliata* below shows a huge-foliaged herbaceous plant which is not commonly seen. It is from the Himalayan foothills and the large leaves are hairy on both sides. It will only survive in a sheltered site, which is exactly what is provided for it in this garden.

The huge hairy leaves of *Bergenia ciliata.*

Not everything is on a huge scale. A very pretty *Gleditsia triacanthos* 'Ruby Lace', as its name indicates, presents quite a different image, and more delicate plants like *Cimicifuga racemosa*, *Dicentra formosa* 'Langtrees' and *Anemone hybrida* 'Luise Uhink', are just a few of the flowers which add so much charm within the foliage.

Here again knowledgeable care has helped this collector to grow some rare plants in a small space, and it is the owner's eye for foliage which has created a very beautiful and dramatic green garden.

EXOTICS IN A COLD GARDEN The other garden, with a similar aim, is that owned by Myles Challis. He has gone overboard for exotic plants, and in a situation like this cold garden, many would not survive the winter. The answer here, as in Sheila Jackson's garden, has been to grow some of the foreigners in pots, but in this case also to cosset them indoors when winter comes.

The framework of this small garden depends upon hardy but also exotic-looking plants. *Trachycarpus fortunei*, a palm, and *Tetrapanax papyriferus* provide dramatic shapes. *Melianthus major* has wonderful grey-green leaves, serrated and rhythmical. A *Dicksonia antarctica* is equally richly textured, being a tree fern. Bamboos and a banana mix with more well-known foliage forms like rodgersias, ligularias, lysichitum and astilbes. Many powerfully shaped leaves overlap one another. The gardener's experience shows, as these diverse forms and textures provide a unique garden style, into which real exotics are added as they visit for the summer season. The photograph opposite shows gunnera with eucalyptus, bamboo, cannas and other triumphant foliage. This is style in a big way.

Left: Canna 'King Humbert' and *Ensete ventricosum* (banana) are some of the dramatic plants that set the style of the garden.

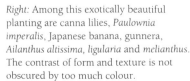

Right: Among this exotically beautiful planting are canna lilies, *Paulownia imperalis*, Japanese banana, gunnera, *Ailanthus altissima, ligularia* and *melianthus*. The contrast of form and texture is not obscured by too much colour.

CASE STUDY
Plants as Designers

Also in town, another pleasingly designed small garden is the long but very narrow one owned and planned by Lucy Gent. In this garden, too, it is the unique 'eye' of the designer which presents many unfamiliar plants in a most appetizing way.

THE LAYOUT The garden is very narrow, being only 5m (16ft) wide, but it is over 40m (132ft) long. The layout is deceptively simple. A narrow, stone-paved, off-centre path leads the way beneath the dense canopy of tall old yew, so you enter the garden from darkness, drawn towards the light, as the glory of the plants stretches before you in the sunshine. Drawn on along the aisle, the visitor halts at crossings. As the garden is so narrow, if there were no pauses the likeness to a railway carriage could be unfortunately apt, but this has been cleverly avoided by 'transepts', which halt forward movement. The path itself stops at the first crossing and from there a small lawn leads on to a hedged sanctum beneath a tree canopy, this time of an old knotted pyracantha. To enter the third garden the way is further off-centre, along one side. Here another path, of tiles, follows the wall beside more grass and wall plants. Just when it appears that this is the end and a most beautiful multi-stemmed *Cercidiphyllum japonicum* asserts itself, yet another small enclave of this final garden is discovered, with a lengthy wooden seat stretching effectively across the end wall. The body can rest where the eye rests.

Seats are sited in all the transition areas, but these are no nostalgic, flowery bowers. The density of the planting on either side, gloriously

Entering a dark sanctuary between clipped box sentinels, there is an inviting glimpse beyond the *Eleagnus* hedge. *Ceanothus repens, Hebe* 'Quicksilver' and a collection of small ferns grow in containers.

scented and brocade-rich with foliage and flower, enfolds the seats. A centrally sited ceramic pot by Jeny Jones, one of many sculptural ceramics in the garden, is wittily planted with *Heuchera cylindrica* 'Pewter Moon', which picks up the carbon blackness of the glazed pot, in sympathetic rather than contrast mode. Everything stops here. There is much to look at. Shrubs like *Camellia* 'Leonard Messel', *Carpenteria californica*, *Ceanothus* 'Autumnal Blue', *Corylopsis pauciflora* and small trees, *Sorbus hupehensis obtusa* and *Gleditsia triacanthos* 'Ruby Lace', provide substance.

THE PLANTING Every small space is planted. This could so easily be a confused rough-and-tumble, but not so. With unerring eye and a collector's knowledge, Lucy has planted aconitum with pale magenta *Allium cernuum*, a gently pink astrantia and the maroon foliage of *Bergenia* 'Abendglut'. Restrained use of silver foliage with cream and pale blues weave in and out of one another. Intense, light-blue-flowered *Geranium wallichianum* 'Buxtons Variety' and grey-foliaged *Sedum telephium* 'Rupertii', with its pale yellow curd-like florets, work beautifully with the foliage of early flowering *Paeonia mlokosewitschii*. These, plus a dash of cool yellow *Lilium* 'La Bohème', are typical of her sensitive colour grouping. In other areas, orange tiger lilies and alstroemeria are glowingly successful when marked by cream-flowered *Campanula alliarifolia*, dark red heuchera foliage and an intense blue delphinium, 'Alice Artindale'.

Everywhere clematis are allowed to cascade amongst the shrubs and perennials, through summer and autumn, threading their way, literally, amongst the gold, as does the rich blue *Clematis* x *jackmanii* with *Rudbeckia maxima*. Other clematis, like the herbaceous *C.* x *eriostemon* 'Columbine', x *jackmanii* 'Alba', the evergreen *armandii*, and a collection of the pretty, late summer-flowering viticellas including 'Alba Luxurians', thread themselves everywhere. Sometimes they wrap themselves into climbing roses and at others they consort with the shrub collection.

This is an interesting mix of shrubs chosen for charm of foliage and flower, stylish habit or rarity. The low *Dorycnium hirsutum* is silvery and velvet textured. At the same level, *Pinus sylvestris* 'Beuvronensis' is a green, spiky ball shape. *Corokia virgata* is stiffly erect, has white-backed leaves and orange berries, whereas *Styrax japonica* has a graceful habit and produces hanging, white bell-shaped flowers.

And yet nothing is too predictable. A vibrant and hardy red *Dahlia* 'Bishop of Llandaff' and *Tropaeolum* 'Ken Aslett' are risks of colour and plant association which more conservative designers might have avoided. Traditional applecarts of familiar pink, pale blue and silver colour schemes are not often upset, but the designer's aesthetic flair makes her take nothing for granted and always question accepted norms. Choosing foliage patterns and valuing the shapes of plants helps to link the whole group. *Cimicifuga racemosa atropurpurea* and *C. r.* 'Brunette' are both present but are subtly different, just as *Hydrangea sargentii* and *H. villosa* have subtle differences. The leaves of these plants, whether slightly

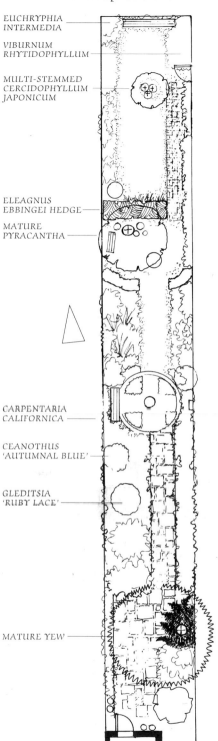

EUCHRYPHIA INTERMEDIA

VIBURNUM RHYTIDOPHYLLUM

MULTI-STEMMED CERCIDOPHYLLUM JAPONICUM

ELEAGNUS EBBINGEI HEDGE

MATURE PYRACANTHA

CARPENTARIA CALIFORNICA

CEANOTHUS 'AUTUMNAL BLUE'

GLEDITSIA 'RUBY LACE'

MATURE YEW

Plants as Designers
A subtle design for a long narrow garden. Changes of character occur at crossings, tempting the visitor to pause.

Above: Delicately beautiful foliage of
Cotinus coggygria 'Grace'.

Below: Sanguisorba obtusa demands
attention, standing out from the soft
colours around it.

feathered and coloured darkish red, or simply ovate, long and silvered grey velvet, provide foils and contrasts. This is the style of planting in this lovely garden. Despite having such narrow widths to work with, the result is one of generous, flowing planting with no sense at all of being restricted by considerations of space.

Always keeping an eye out for new species or hybrids, Lucy's discoveries are passed on, as seen in the garden designed by her which is featured in Chapter 9. Some perceptive variations on the familiar have been chosen. There is a *Hamamelis intermedia* 'Carmine Red', which is not commonly seen. A *Rubus* species grows well, but is so recently collected that it is as yet unnamed. A remarkable 2m (7ft) *Euphorbia sikkimense* grows in shade. It has rich red early shoots and yellow flowers in late summer. *Cercis canadensis* 'Forest Pansy' is not yet seen everywhere, though I suspect that, like the yellow *Robinia pseudoacacia* 'Frisia', it soon will be. But the subtlety of this designer can be seen in the choice of dusky, red-foliaged plants like *Cotinus* 'Grace'. This shrub, though still basically red leaved, has an almost slate-soft greyness with a turquoise overtone. The photograph above shows this very well. Just as refreshing is a heuchera, obviously a buddy of *Heuchera* 'Palace Purple'. This one, mentioned earlier, is silver mottled and appropriately named *Heuchera cylindrica* 'Pewter Moon'. I must also refer to a plant which I failed to recognize at all and am utterly won over by. This is *Begonia* 'Burle Marx', which Lucy has grown in a shaded site in a pot. It has richly incised leaves with a grainy, brown-leather texture enhanced by sprays of off-white flowers.

The many pots in the garden, in which some other unusual specimens are grown, are moved forward when they come into their 'fifteen minutes of fame', as Warhol would have seen it. In the photograph opposite, a view of this garden looking back from the path under the pyracantha shows a variegated clipped box and some of the richly mixed planting of the border. *Heuchera cylindrica* 'Pewter Moon' can be seen in its basalt-black pot, and large white and blue agapanthus reap the benefit of being associated with scented-leaved geraniums. But, most noticeable, growing in a pot is an unusual fluffy pink-flowered Japanese burnet (*Sanguisorba obtusa*). The designer is none too pleased with this, as she finds the pink rather chemical. Like some of her collection, it was of interest, but may well be offered a new home next year. It is typical of her collector's instinct that she should give it a home for a season, but as it failed to satisfy it must relinquish its space to a more appreciated performer next year. Because of such incisiveness, this is a garden which is creatively coherent and gives a great deal of pleasure.

UNUSUAL HERBACEOUS PLANTS

Agapanthus campanulatus 'Stella Thomas'
Allium triquetrum
Anaphalis 'Nubigena'
Anemone hybrida 'Luise Uhink'
A. h. 'Whirlwind'
Anthemis 'Tetworth'
Artemisia canescens
Asarum europeaum
Begonia 'Burle Marx'
B. ciliata
Boykinia aconitifolia
Cephalaria gigantea
Cimicifuga racemosa 'Brunette'
C. r. 'Purpurea'
Cirsium rivulare atropurpureum
Clematis eriostemon
C. recta purpurea
Diascia anastrepta
Dicentra formosa 'Langtrees'
Dierama pumilum
Epilobium angustifolium album
E. chlorifolium
Ephedra gerardiana
Equisetum robustum
Eremurus 'Shelford Hybrids'
Eryngium bourgattii
E. variifolium
E. zabellii 'Violetta'
Erysimum 'Wenlock Beauty'
Euphorbia characias 'Dwarf Form'
E. griffithii 'Dixter'
E. longifolia
E. martinii
Fibigia clypeata
Galtonia viridiflora

Geranium macrorrhizum 'Album'
G. renardii
G. tuberosum
G. wallichianum 'Buxton's Variety'
Geum 'Coppertone'
Gladiolus byzantinus
Hemerocallis 'Black Magic'
H. 'Citrina'
H. 'Golden Chimes'
Heuchera cylindrica 'Green Finch'
H. c. 'Pewter Moon'
H. c. 'Snowstorm'
Hosta undulata
H. ventricosa
H. 'Zounds'
Iris 'Florentina'
I. germanica dwarf 'Blue Denim'
I. g. dwarf 'Green Spot'
I. sibirica 'Langthorne's Pink'
I. s. 'Snow Queen'
I. unguicularis
Isatis tinctoria
Knautia macedonica
Kniphofia galpinii
K. 'Little Maid'
Linum narbonense 'Heavenly Blue'
Lobelia 'Valida'
Lupinus 'Argentea'
Lysimachia clethroides
Melica ciliata
Nepeta nervosa
Omphalodes cappadocica
Pachyphragma macrophylla
Penstemon 'Alice Hindley'
Phygelius 'Moonraker'
P. 'Winchester Fanfare'
Plantago major 'Rosularis'

Sanguisorba obtusa
Scabiosa caucasica
S. 'Miss Wilmott'
Schizostylis coccinea 'Alba'
Sedum maximum 'Atropurpureum'
S. telephium 'Rupertii'
Veronica spicata 'Incana'

For shade and semi-shade

Aconitum septentrionale 'Ivorine'
Arisaema speciosum
Astilbe 'Sinensis Pumila'
Astrantia major 'Rubra'
Brunnera macrophylla 'Hadspen Cream'
B. m. 'Langtrees'
Darmera peltata
Digitalis ciliata
Epimedium pinnatum colchicum
E. youngeanum 'Niveum'
Euphorbia sikkimensis
Geranium phaeum 'Album'
Helleborus foetidus 'Variegatum'
H. f. 'Wester Flisk'
Hosta 'Eric Smith Hybrid'
H. 'Golden Nakaiana'
H. plantaginea
Iris foetidissima citrina
I. f. 'Variegata'
Lamium 'Cannon's Gold'
Primula vialii
Reynoutria japonica 'Spectabilis'
Smilacina racemosa
Tanacetum 'Sissinghurst White'
Telekia speciosa
Tiarella wherryi
Tricyrtis hirta var. *alba*
Uvularia grandiflora

7 · Mainly for Looking At

'Just as a frame can make or mar a painting, the front garden can add distinction or welcoming charm to your house'

Mainly for looking at? All gardens are for looking at. Of course they are. But some are for looking rather than spending much time in. They are usually front gardens, where the demands made of the planting are that it has to be all year round and should be easy to maintain. The gardens described here are as different from one another as the houses to which they belong: a front garden should usually be in character with the period or style of the house.

In terms of the hard landscaping and structure, these gardens must be practical. They should also suit the surrounding architectural style. Just as a frame can make or mar a painting, the front garden can add distinction or welcoming charm to your house, whereas ignored grass, wild seeded michaelmas daisies, shapeless lilac and a neglected, struggling rose can make it drab and uninviting.

The simplest ways of making an attractive frontage are either to refuse to acknowledge the road, by blocking it out completely with dense, evergreen, dusty hedges like privet, or to display the house rather baldly, surrounding it with a manicured lawn, a drive, a central bed for annual bedding and low linked-chain-and-post fencing which, dare I say, would look more appropriate around a grave.

If, however, you feel more ambitious and want to display your home beautifully, treat this frontage as a small gem of design which needs no patio, seating, compost or utility space. The main constraint is likely to be the need for a drive to the garage and an entrance to the front door. Dustbins have to be collected, outdoor meters read and post delivered, as well as friends welcomed. After that, privacy may be a consideration. But one factor is probable: you are unlikely to want to spend too much time mowing grass, tending shrubs or trimming a privet hedge, which can require eight cuts in a season.

THE ROLE OF THE CAR

In most cities, cars can no longer stand in front of the house for free. Metering and car parking tokens cost money, so if you can get your car off the road it will be a considerable saving. Bear in mind when planning for this that you also have to get the car out on to the road again. Small front gardens do not often have room for a one-way, semi-circular drive, so if you have to reverse out do not impede your vision with shrubs, and do provide plenty of room for misjudgements. There is usually no real need for piers on either side of a drive unless there is a brick or timber boundary. The average car is 4.3 x 1.7m (14 x 5 ½ft), so you may not have room for turning, or indeed for two cars plus pedestrian access. In such cases there are a few problems to overcome.

Sample Plans

The drawings show four different drives in small front gardens. Fig 1 shows a very small frontage. Parking meters were being installed in the area. The owner wanted to retain some privacy and half enclose the space, and raised brick planters helped to achieve this. The planting had to be fairly low but, as a focus, an attractive specimen acer *Acer palmatum* 'Dissectum Viridis' was planted in the corner. As this is not a windswept area and the maple has done well, draping softly over the brick wall. The plants are all easy to maintain. *Parahebe catarractae* and *P. lyallii*, *Hebe* 'Margret', *Armeria maritima* 'Alba', *Achillea* 'King Edward' and small *Artemisia schmidtiana* 'Nana' provide shapes and colours. *Sisyrinchium striatum* 'Variegatum' adds some grass-like foliage, and *Sedum lidakense* trails over the side with *Phlox subulata* 'White Delight', *Campanula muralis* and alpine hardy geraniums. Small spring bulbs like *Iris reticulata*, dwarf narcissus and *Scilla sibirica* add early brightness.

Fig 2 (overleaf) shows a very simple arrangement where the tarmaced drive provides good visibility on one side. However, nothing could be done about the other because of the neighbours' wall. It was therefore decided to make a wide curve where the drive meets the road. Beside the front door a small area of tiles does away with the need for a separate path, and all the planting is reserved to go around this and the house. Only a specimen *Pyrus salicifolia* 'Pendula' breaks the lawn shape. This

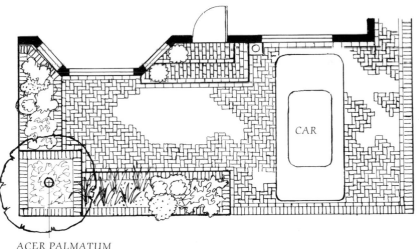

ACER PALMATUM
'DISSECTUM VIRIDIS'

Fig 1 A very narrow frontage provides space for the car and retains some privacy.

ELEVATION

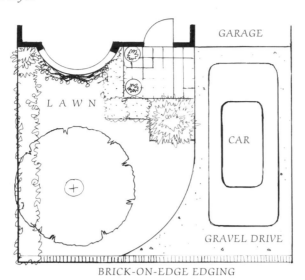

Fig 2 Access and visibility are good even though the entrance is semi-enclosed with planting.

GARAGE

LAWN

CAR

GRAVEL DRIVE

BRICK-ON-EDGE EDGING

tree is here clipped into a mushroom shape so that visibility is not impeded for the car driver.

A more elaborate plan was needed for the front garden and drive shown in Fig 3. Here, there is room for two cars and access is not a problem. A brick path leads from the drive, laid with 'brick-on-edge' in a stretcher bond pattern, to the verandah and around the house. The chosen bricks match the new but old-looking brickwork of the house. Two green lawns add tranquillity and the planting around is simple, with low evergreens like wide-spreading junipers, hebes, *Euonymus fortunei* varieties, *Cistus corbariensis*, *C.* 'Silver Pink' and *Viburnum davidii*. The owner was keen to keep some areas free for seasonal colour, so spaces were left for spring bulbs and summer annuals. The drive is concrete aggregate and trouble free. The one tree is a columnar *Ginkgo biloba*, a tall

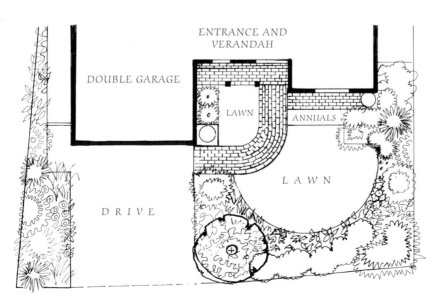

ENTRANCE AND VERANDAH

DOUBLE GARAGE

LAWN

ANNUALS

LAWN

DRIVE

Fig 3 On a larger scale, the cars have space and the house has an intimate front garden.

Fig 4 A holly hedge separates the house from the road, leaving a thin strip for access and space for a car.

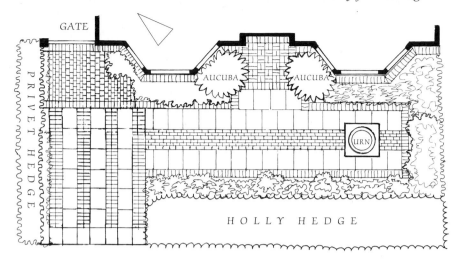

and narrow tree which is fairly uncommon and has a rather distinguished air.

In the fourth plan, Fig 4, the scope was very limited. The house is over one hundred years old and is a terraced home made from mellow brick. There is little room for plants, so the hard landscaping had added importance. Soft yellow brick was chosen and simulated stone flags blended well. The narrow space is edged by a beautiful but dark 1.8m (6ft) high clipped holly hedge. There is no garage, but there is sufficient room to get the car off the road. The hedge reduces much of the nutritive value of the soil, so this is reconditioned annually. Despite this, it has been a simple matter to select plants for the site. Ferns like the male fern (*Dryopteris filix-mas*) cope with most conditions. A hart's tongue fern (*Asplenium scolopendrium* 'Crispum') adds a glossy, lighter green and is doing well. The reliable *Euphorbia robbiae* is spreading, and weaving around it are two lamiums, *Lamium maculatum* 'Beacon Silver' and *L.m.* 'White Nancy'. Bulbs are invaluable. *Narcissus* 'February Gold' and *N.* 'Hawera' grow near the house. On the side behind the planting urn, *Allium moly* provides bright yellow in late spring, preceded by *Scilla sibirica*. Opposite the house, white, pink and blue *Anemone blanda* flower in early spring. Massed around the paving in summer, busy lizzies (*Impatiens*) are fetching for three months. All of this planting means that fertilizer must be added to the soil soon after the bulbs have flowered to help to restore nourishment. Two matching specimens of *Aucuba crotonifolia* flank the doorway, looking good all year. Finally, as a focal detail central to the path, an urn on a plinth is sited in front of the living room window.

The plans show just four types of front garden with provision for car standing as an integrated part of the design. Drives must always be carefully constructed and are best laid by experts. Tarmac, rolled gravel and concrete are all possible materials. Smaller units like concrete bricks, dry laid in a herringbone pattern, or granite setts laid in alternative patterns, are other attractive possibilities.

SEASONAL PLANTS FOR CONTAINERS

Ageratum houstonianum
Alyssum
Atriplex hortensis
Begonia semperflorens
Bulbs
Calendula officinalis
Cheiranthus
Coleus
Dimorpotheca
Felicia amelloides
Fuchia
Gazania
Helichrysum microphyllum
Heliotrope
Impatiens walleriana
Lobelia erinus
Nicotiana sylvestris
Pelargonium
Petunia
Phyllitis scolopendrium
Polyanthus
Verbena
Viola

Apart from the needs of the car, there is always the importance of easy access to the front door for visitors and for services, so footpaths must be supplied. Rather unusually, this was not so for the house in the photograph below, which shows how the garden of this modern home looked originally.

CASE STUDY

Planned Geometry in a Front Garden

The rectangular architecture of this modern housing development is vigorously emphasized with black and white paint. The line of the houses along the road is strongly horizontal as there are no pitched roofs. These parallel horizontals dominate the street in a dramatic way. The houses are mostly on two levels, each with an integral garage and car parking space. Initially there was no front path. Instead, access to the front door was via the drive, where the car stands, making it necessary to squeeze past. The rest of the front garden was a square area of rather unruly grass which was vaguely planted with shrubs. As the courtyard behind the house is paved there was little cause to introduce grass at the front – storing a mower for one small patch seemed pointless. Consequently, a new plan was needed which would provide a front path and do away with the grass. It also required a more modern approach, geometrically in sympathy with the architectural style of the house.

THE LAYOUT   The plan (opposite) for the new garden shows how a design was worked out accordingly. The first essential being the path meant that there would also be a strip of planting between it and the drive. This left a rectangular space on the other side which included an existing conifer and a *Robinia pseudoacacia* 'Frisia'. In deference to the geometry of the house, this was divided up by straight lines which formed overlapping rectangles. To reinforce these, old railway timbers

The original front garden where the only access to the front door was via the hard standing for the car.

Planned Geometry in a Front Garden
The top plan shows the layout with the path to the door and the garden divided. The second plan shows planting softening the geometry.

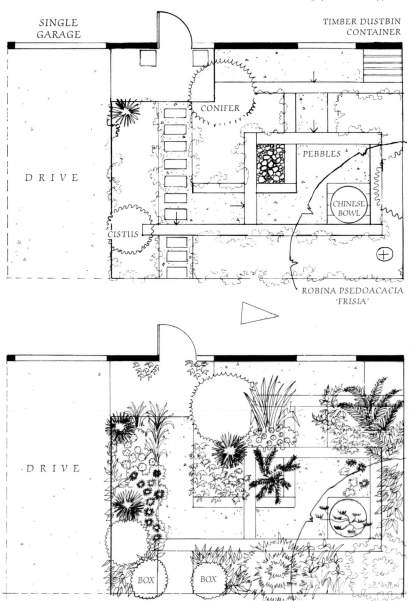

SINGLE GARAGE

TIMBER DUSTBIN CONTAINER

CONIFER

PEBBLES

CHINESE BOWL

DRIVE

CISTUS

ROBINA PSEDOACACIA 'FRISIA'

DRIVE

BOX

BOX

edged the planting beds and bordered the L-shaped access path. Thus opportunities occurred for textural change and a space for a timber plinth. Grasping the chance to make a new footpath to the door meant that people were no longer of a lower order than the car. The photograph overleaf shows how this layout worked before any of the plants were put in.

MATERIALS The materials chosen to look good with the sleepers were gravel, pavers and cobblestones. Plain areas of gravel balanced the design and also provided access. Where the railway sleepers overlap, an area for rounded cobbles, framed by the timber, was planted with a specimen dwarf pine. Opposing this is the square plinth, on which is displayed a

This photograph shows how the garden was relaid. The old tangled grass has been removed and the layout pattern links with the geometry of the house and provides planting beds which are easier to keep under control.

A path for direct access to the front door has now been provided.

Tiny conifers, seen here at five years old, grow through slits in the plastic beneath the gravel.

very wide and shallow reproduction Chinese bowl. Due to the slight change in levels, one of the sleepers crosses the gravel as a shallow step down. The gravel is underlaid with a woven plastic sheeting, allowing water to penetrate but retarding weeds. In one small corner cross-slits were made so that some very dwarf conifers could be planted. These were *Juniperus communis* 'Compressa', *Chamaecyparis obtusa* 'Nana Intermedia' and *Thuja orientalis* 'Minima Glauca'. They can be seen in the photograph above.

THE PLANTING The planting is mostly of low, colourful shrubs, many of which look good all year round. As can be seen in the photograph overleaf, these include conifers like *Taxus baccata* 'Fastigiata Robusta' for its dark, vertical line, and *Cedrus deodara* 'Golden Horizon', which is a

very slow-growing cedar with a cascading, fair-haired silhouette. A very large, healthy *Phormium tenax* was also chosen. Colour is provided with a pruned red berberis and *Santolina chamaecyparissus*. Varieties of *Euonymus fortunei*, variegated ivies and *Potentilla fruticosa* 'Primrose Beauty' are also easy to care for. Two clipped balls of box mark the entrance path to the garden.

As with other front gardens, bulbs and annuals add great vitality at different times of the year. In spring *Iris reticulata* and *Tulipa tarda* flank the path and primroses, pinks and campanulas seasonally follow through. Added to these, annuals provide colour in the summer. The

Colour in this small front garden is achieved mainly with foliage. Some of this is evergreen and all of it is simple to maintain.

104

A wide, shallow Chinese bowl stands on a timber base which is flush with the gravel.

Chinese container, seen in the photograph above, is filled with white marguerites (argyranthemums), and white violas, which surround the permanently planted blue abies. At most times of the year there is colour in the garden, but it is foliage as well as flowers which provides it.

CASE STUDY

In Which Plants are Responsible

The small front garden shown in the photograph on page 107 is quite different in style. There was no drawn plan for this and no alterations were needed to the existing hard landscaping, so the owners had only to choose plants and plant them. The original maintained lawn had proved to be an irritant to the owners, as it never seemed to be very healthy and suffered from *fusarium* patches. (This is a fungus disease, and when infected, circular patches of lawn die off and become a brown-yellow colour). It was also quite a palaver to bring the mower through the house to the front. In addition, an unattractive concrete retaining wall made from drab grey breeze-blocks was far from pretty. As a result, it was decided to replace the grass with low evergreens interspersed with non-staking herbaceous plants which arise or subside as their turn comes around. The house itself is already prettily framed with *Rosa* 'Handel', a bi-coloured climber, and a mass of red and pink roses with lavender footings around the bay window. It was decided to keep all of these.

THE PLANTING The early season begins with spring bulbs and hellebores, which precede the magnanimity of *Magnolia stellata*. This

slow-growing magnolia is starred with flowers in early spring at the same time as the primulas and pulsatillas bloom. This is a very sunny site and as the summer wears on the flowers increase. Early on, small rhododendrons – 'Bow Bells', 'Chikor' and the tiny 'Moerheim' – do well in this acidic soil, shaded by larger shrubs. They contribute bright colour, which is later endorsed by the roses 'The Fairy' and 'Queen Mother' (both pink). *Weigela florida* 'Foliis Purpureis' adds dark red leaves around pink tubular flowers. *Cistus corbariensis* is a larger, rounded evergreen and though the flowers are white the buds are wine-pink. Later on, the cold blue-pink and red flower theme is picked up by *Fuchsia* 'Tom Thumb', the flowers of which have a rich red calyx around violet-purple petals.

The herbaceous plants which do well are all easy ones. They include a clump of small *Hemerocallis* 'Stella d'Oro', *Euphorbia griffithii* 'Fireglow', a mid-blue agapanthus, *Schizostylis coccinea* 'Mrs Hegarty', *Heuchera* 'Shere Variety' and *Bergenia purpurascens*. None of these needs either staking or tying. Occasional deadheading of flowerheads or removal of dead foliage is all that is necessary. The day lilies and euphorbia add some warm colour, but as this is a hot and sunny garden the cooler hues are really valued.

It is the low, small shrubs on which the rest of the *mélange* depends. A small *Pinus mugo* var. *Pumilio*, pretty red-leaved *Pittosporum tenuifolium* 'Purpureum', *Hebe albicans*, *Lavandula stoechas* and *Salvia officinalis* 'Purpurascens' are there all year round, while the edging of

helianthemum, *Geranium* 'Laurence Flatman', *Phlox subulata* 'Oakington' and *Anthemis cupaniana* carry colour down at ground level. This very dense planting makes any weed think twice about competing.

The wall itself needed covering. A narrow strip of soil below it has proved sufficient to support valerian, osteospermum, pinks and a small hypericum, all of which conceal the base. From above *Cotoneaster dammeri* (which is regularly pruned), *Hedera helix* 'Green Feather', another ivy, *Juniperus squamata* 'Blue Carpet' and variegated *Vinca minor* hang over. The photograph on page 106 shows how this is working.

Something is in flower each month, even in winter, and the garden is always attractive with contrasting forms and colour. As it was planted and is maintained by the owners they know how to care for it, which involves detailed attention about four times a year. Otherwise, occasional deadheading or light pruning is sufficient.

Frequent interest from passers-by has increased social intercourse in the neighbourhood, which was an unexpected pleasure. Gardens can be most welcoming.

CASE STUDY
Simply Effective

The original front garden plan shown here is quite a contrast, being informal and with a meandering path made from granite kerb stones of varying lengths. The basic flooring is gravel and upon this the granite rests immovably. To one side of this double-fronted garden ivy is an easily maintained ground cover beneath dark red *Prunus pissardii* 'Nigra'. It is clipped concentrically around a neatly circular planting of bergenias. To the other side a group of three granite slabs amongst the gravel has provided a simple focus for different hostas, which seem to remain unviolated as slugs don't much like gravel. *Nepeta* 'Six Hills Giant' and hellebores complete this very simple but effective scheme which was designed by Lucy Gent.

Simply Effective
This is an unusual garden, fronted by gravel and granite slabs rather than lawn, with selected planting.

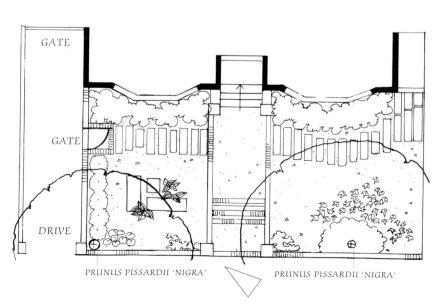

GATE

GATE

DRIVE

PRUNUS PISSARDII 'NIGRA'   PRUNUS PISSARDII 'NIGRA'

CASE STUDY
Elegant Sufficiency

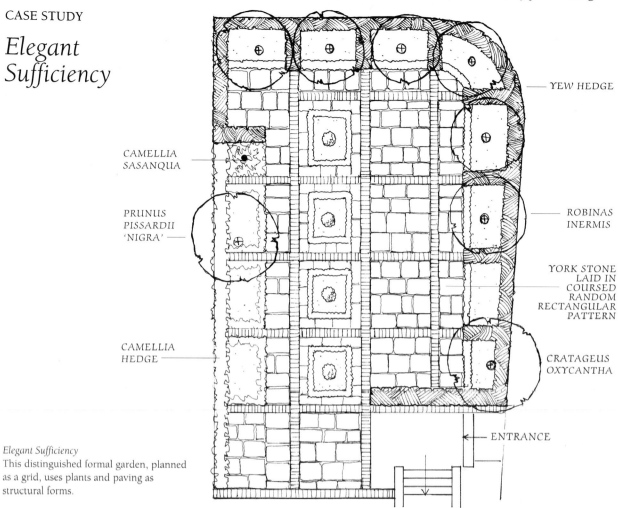

CAMELLIA
SASANQUA

PRUNUS
PISSARDII
'NIGRA'

CAMELLIA
HEDGE

YEW HEDGE

ROBINAS
INERMIS

YORK STONE
LAID IN
COURSED
RANDOM
RECTANGULAR
PATTERN

CRATAGEUS
OXYCANTHA

ENTRANCE

Elegant Sufficiency
This distinguished formal garden, planned
as a grid, uses plants and paving as
structural forms.

'Any more would be needless superfluity.' Thus George Bernard Shaw could have described the next garden. Though on a grander scale and very sophisticated, this is actually planned on very simple principles by the designer, Victor Shanley. If you look at the plan above and photograph overleaf you will see a simple but quite large rectangular space in which all the linear patterns lie in parallels. It is a balanced and rhythmical use of geometric shapes and patterns within a set space.

THE PLANTING The street boundaries are furnished by formal yew hedging, which backs planting beds around the garden, rather as buttresses would support a brick wall. Within these are rectangular alcoves filled with selected planting. A row of mopheaded acacias, *Robinia pseudoacacia* 'Inermis', line up above head height, insulating the garden from the surrounding buildings and road traffic. On the side adjacent to the neighbours the hedging is equally darkly evergreen, but more informal, being of *Camellia japonica* 'Alba Simplex' which has beautiful single white flowers.

Small Gardens with Style

Throughout the garden a simple colour scheme dominated by green and enhanced by white is charmingly effective. Green provides the structure but in variations of dark and light. The yew and camellia are a very dark theme, picked up by the painted planters. But the box hedging is a bright, cheerful mid-green and by edging at a lower level acts as an inner frame for the whole garden. Whites glow within the yew alcoves. *Rosa* 'Iceberg' flowers reliably through the summer, supported by delicately pale blue rosemary. Light blue *Lavandula angustifolia* 'Munstead' picks up this theme and marguerites, white lilies and foxgloves add verve, underplanted with *Lamium maculatum* 'White Nancy'. Small-leaved green ivy, *Hedera helix* 'Pointer', plays a part and annually, white busy lizzies (*Impatiens*) and white and lime green

The layout of this elegant garden is seen clearly from the first floor. The mop-headed acacias surround the street boundaries and box hedging provides sculptural detail.

This photograph shows the attention given to detail, with the brick pattern running between enclosed boxed beds.

nicotianas continue the theme. In spring, massed white *Narcissus* 'Actaea' with blue scillas look very pretty, followed by quantities of *Tulipa* 'White Triumphator'. The planting is elegantly restrained and suits the garden well, showing that we do not always have to use every colour in the spectrum to create a beautiful garden.

SHAPES AND FORMS Shapes dominate this garden. Clipped box as pyramids or domes are lined up geometrically and have tremendous sculptural presence. They are static within painted Versailles cube-shaped tubs or strictly square box hedging, and line up with great precision.

This is the key to the garden's success. As seen on the plan, a grid pattern of old stock bricks creates squares which are either hedged with box as described, or filled in with random lengths of paving running laterally. Some of the brick lines of the grid pierce the box-edged border on one side of the garden, as in the photograph above. This subtly echoes the converse shape on the other side, where it is yew hedge which intrudes into the garden space, enclosing the squared planting bed. This attention to detail is characteristic of Victor's work and, like many of his ideas, worth emulating.

Looking at the gardens described in this chapter, you will see that it is possible to devise quite different ideas which can make houses look individual and welcoming within a wide range of expense and effort.

111

8 · Modern Formality

'The human spirit is such that we must always be devising new thoughts for old needs.'

What many people want from gardens is a world of comfortable security, in which unchallenging familiarity is perennially reassuring. The great gardens were indeed marvellous. The Lutyens-Jekyll association, for example, produced creations of quality and immense beauty – no wonder they have been so inspirational. House styles, too, often hark back to a 'golden age' of family villas, with intimations of rurality. But we have been through huge social and cultural changes, and life is no longer as it appears to have been. Even nostalgia is not what it used to be; television has seen to that. Now, in the terminal stages of the twentieth century, should we not look forward? Le Corbusier and the Bauhaus were at their most influential over half a century ago, but are still thought of as avant-garde. Many 'isms' later we are still drawn to a 'utopia' of middle-class prosperity with gardens which were seen as diminutive estates. I am no different, and confess to such an admiration of Lutyens' hard landscaping that it is difficult to free myself and move away from him. He is rightly very influential.

THE 'NEW' DESIGNING

The 'new' designing of the post-war years was influenced by developments in the visual arts. There was a need to discard finally the refuge of historical derivation and see the contemporary garden as a functional adjunct to the living spaces created by modern architects. The aim was to provide roomy outdoor places which were to be enjoyed as part of the domestic experience, rather than a mini-landscaped refuge with 'cottagey' associations. Some of the work of this time now seems unfriendly and harsh in its geometry and use of material. But there is a time for everything, and I suspect that in a couple of decades pierced concrete walls, simple spacious gardens and slim metal pergola piers will have a revival, much as 'art deco' has today. For the public of the time, such boldness was too uncomfortable for domestic gardens. It seemed acceptable in public places, but the one area to which it was directed, the personal private garden, did not take to it.

The rise of reprinted William Morris wallpapers and the success of Laura Ashley cottons shows the direction of public taste. In a nuclear-threatened world this is not surprising; the greening of conscience is vital and has led to many changes. However, nostalgia should not be tyrannical. Nineteenth-century society was socially divisive and rapaciously devoured natural resources. A 'golden age' in which elegant shepherdesses posed against a pre-Raphaelite sprinkling of wildflowers was always a sentimentalized view of this world. We cannot afford to be like that today. Throughout the book I have returned time and again to the *function* of a garden, that is to the practical needs of the owner. Though this book is about style, failing to refer to the fundamentals would make the designs pointless. 'Hard-nosed' constraints are the scaffolding on which good gardens are planned, and this is increasingly how they should be thought of in the future.

THE WAY FORWARD

Yet they need not be quite as dauntingly spare as those of the post-war years. A well-worked layout on simple geometric lines does not mean that a garden cannot be lovely and charming. The textures, scents and colours of the plant material are available as never before, both in their original species form and with the new hybrid vigour and disease-resistance, all of which would have been invaluable to gardeners of the past.

Another influence upon contemporary designing is an enormous respect for classic Japanese gardens. In our recent Western, bountiful, 'technicolour' planting we had lost sight of simple tranquillity, and the asymmetric but balanced gardens of Japan, with studied use of hard materials and ruthless selection of plants, have created a distilled aesthetic of harmony which is increasingly influential. The simple economy of line and space suggest a contemplative silence. There is meaning behind these designs: they are as embodied with Buddhist philosophies as Byzantine icons are with Christianity. It is impossible to recreate them, but one can observe and try to gain insight into the philosophy and practice of these garden makers.

So here we are, a wealth of diverse garden experience behind us; with a real need for creative and beautiful outdoor domestic spaces; new, tough, but attractive materials available; plants freely crossing the globe like migrating birds; and we have another century in which to press forward.

Architecturally, the labels 'Constructivism', 'Functionalism', 'Post Modernist', 'New Classicist' and 'International Style' can be very confusing, but basically the main conclusions which are influencing modern garden design are that forms and spaces should be simple and unpretentious. Clarity of geometric form is desirable as a balance to the waywardness of plant growth. Abstract forms can take the shape of Naum Gabo's parabolas or organically inspired shapes after Henry Moore. Simplicity is valued. Boulders, rocks and pebbles, inspired by Japan, now take on sculptural importance in the space of the garden. New use is made of timber, concrete, glass, rubber and metals, and reconstituted stuffs are sought with 'saving the planet' in mind. But the overall demand must be that of the human spirit. New ideas are always alarming – they are seen as threatening old values. Wrong. This need not be. The human spirit is such that we must always be devising new thoughts for old needs. But gardens do also need to reach out to the onlooker and be 'friendly'. And then, one day, they will become so familiar that they are sought after. Should the media take up the gauntlet and actually show us innovative garden designs, then the whole process of acceptance could be speeded up.

In this chapter I have chosen gardens which are attractive, welcoming and planned on modern lines. There are differences of interest and style, but all are contemporary and tranquil.

CASE STUDY
The Slate Garden

The plan opposite is of a recently designed garden which uses a superb slate from Cumbria. The design consists of a centred small lawn surrounded on three sides by a small water-course. Slate paving encloses these, making a pleasant circular walk. There is a partially enclosed alcove for seating and an open, stepped plinth in the opposite corner from which an imposing sculpture by Michael Archer dominates the garden. This was created specially for the garden and is totally in sympathy with the materials and formality of the design. The extremely simple layout is based uncompromisingly on rectangles. Slate is perfectly suited to the style as it can be cut and laid with linear precision. It has been sawn into random lengths in four different widths, and these are laid in parallel courses across the garden so that each area is united as part of the whole. The surface of the slabs is a roughened 'flamed' texture which is safe in all weathers and presents an opaque, jade-green surface. As this is a particularly beautiful stone with varying shades of colour and rich bedding patterns, thin strips of highly polished, honed slate have been inserted across the front path, offering a richer colour and reflective surface. Beyond the grass these lines follow through within the paving between the trees, making much of their existence and linking the garden areas together.

Green slate is ideal for a modern garden. It is extremely strong and can be cut with diamond precision, which suits the spare, 'hard-edged' designs of contemporary architecture. Though it has in the past been used in a more 'rustic' manner, as the building material for dry stone walls, its true beauty is best revealed when it is worked with the accuracy of fine marble. Paradoxically, this is an ancient rock in geological terms yet it performs superbly in the modern idiom, and the palely cool green provides a sophisticated surface stone for a contemporary town garden.

SYMMETRY AND PLANTING From one view the design is almost symmetrical, as seen in the plan opposite. Raised planters fashioned from large, strong slabs of slate are of matching height and act as theatrical 'wings', presenting the three striking white-barked birches (*Betula utilis* var. *jacquemontii*) in the spotlight. Behind these, very simple planting of massed ferns (*Athyrium filix-femina*) are backed by a dark, fairly large-leaved ivy, *Hedera helix* 'Montgomery', and at the foot of the trees are collars of very small ferns, *Adiantum pedatum*, *Blechnum penna-marina* and

Polypodium vulgare. Flanking the stage are twinned specimens of *Juniperus sabina* 'Tamariscifolia', a neat conifer with overlapping concentric growth, grown in the raised beds with viburnums, osmanthus and acers.

As already mentioned, from one view the garden layout is uncomplicated and very nearly symmetrical, but from the sitting area it is quite different in character, as can be seen in the photograph overleaf. This is an enclosed, semi-shaded area where there is room to sit with good company and a glass or two. From here the scene is asymmetrical, with large emphatic planting on one side but lower, more relaxed plants on the other. All is viewed through a frame; above, the lacquer-red pergola supporting trails of wisteria, and below, fringed with green pygmy bamboo.

COLOUR THEMES This red is echoed around the courtyard with the flowers and foliage of astilbe, dicentra, acers and the dark-red-leaved *Weigela florida* 'Foliis Purpureis'. A carefully introduced claret red appears in *Cirsium rivulare* 'Atropurpureum', *Centaurea ruthenica*, *Lobelia cardinalis* and *Heuchera* 'Red Spangles'. In some parts of the garden the colour edges positively towards purple hues. *Vitis vinifera* 'Purpurea' offers purple-grey foliage colour, rather similar to the grey-purple leaves of the sage *Salvia officinalis* 'Purpurascens'. This in turn links with another

The Slate Garden
A narrow water course separates but links different areas of this peaceful modern town garden. The sculpture is viewed from secluded seating.

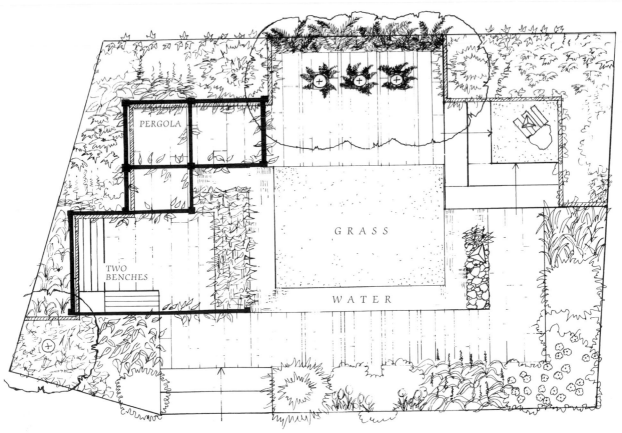

This view from beneath the pergola shows a tranquil modern garden. The sculpture was made for the garden by Michael Dan Archer, and is carved from Cumbrian green slate.

117

sage, *Salvia officinalis* 'Tricolor', which has green, grey, purple and white in its foliage and this, in its turn, associates well with the variegated *Iris pallida* 'Variegata', grown for its grey-and-cream leaves.

Soft grey colour is echoed around the garden, cooling the red and linking with the jade-green tones of the slate. A large *Phormium tenax* dominates on one side; *Allium karataviense* has equally sculptured but far smaller pewter-grey leaves and these are heightened by being placed near to silvered *Stachys byzantina*. Across the entrance path *Salix hastata* 'Wehrhahnii' picks up the silver-grey theme, while in the raised planters the magnificent foliage of *Hosta seiboldiana* adds distinctly blue tones. In this shaded area *Omphalodes cappadocica* emphasizes the blue in spring.

Another view shows the narrow water course which leads around the garden. Restrained planting works sympathetically with the soft blue of the slate.

Other subtle colour changes are made with *Acer platanoides* 'Crimson Sentry', where red now veers towards bronze. In selecting this colour change, some pale yellows settle in comfortably. *Cytisus kewensis*, the grass *Milium effusum* 'Aureum' and a primrose-yellow day lily align themselves with the burnt-orange colour of *Euphorbia griffithii* 'Fireglow'.

But I really designed this as a very green garden. *Acer negundo* 'Elegans', ferns, bamboo, *Hydrangea quercifolia*, *Wisteria macrobotrys*, *Geranium renardii*, *Mitella breweri*, *Heuchera cylindrica* 'Greenfinch' and *Sedum spectabile* 'Autumn Joy' contribute lime, emerald and jade greens. Portuguese laurel, *Viburnum tinus* and the loquat (*Eriobotrya japonica*) add dark and rich textures, while white flowers such as those of *Exochorda macrantha* 'The Bride', *Solanum jasminoides* 'Album' and *Epilobium angustifolium* 'Alba' add lustre.

The water-course is notably simple. It follows the rectangular theme and is not adorned with plants. Only in one small area, where there are flattened, rounded green stones and a bronze pyramid linked to the sculpture, have two water plants been chosen. They are red *Lobelia cardinalis* and a small rush, *Typha minima*. This then is a formal, modern garden which is also tranquil and welcoming.

CASE STUDY

A Garden of Square Roots

Squares, rather than rectangles, are the inspiration for this small garden. It is also a design which belongs wholly to the end of the twentieth century. Designed by Barbara Hunt and named the 'Square Roots' garden, it has a strongly geometric plan using both squares and cubes as design units.

THE LAYOUT The plan overleaf shows how the designer has worked these into the overall square of the garden. Symmetry is all important and the main entrance is central. It leads between two sentinel conifers and beneath a tall 'timber' pergola. Hostas fringe the path on both sides and small domes of clipped box indicate the entrance to the courtyard. The pergola itself is worth detailed attention – it is not what it seems. As well as providing a powerful frame for the entrance, it also carries a hidden water source above head height. From the rafters, water trickles down suspended metal chains on both sides into the adjacent pools. This is a delightfully rococo detail within such a formal space. The pools are quiet, square stretches of water with water lilies at rest on the surface and golden fish gleaming below. Once in the main courtyard one finds a very comfortable open space with a ramped entrance at one end and a square-based gazebo at the other. Immediately opposite the pergola, along the strong central axis, is a silvered cube fountain. Here the movement of water enlivens the static geometry of the design, flowing over the top of the cube into a basin and emerging from three chutes, made from old ridge tiles, into a long, low water trough. More clipped box provides domes in a sea of helichrysum, as they merge into purple

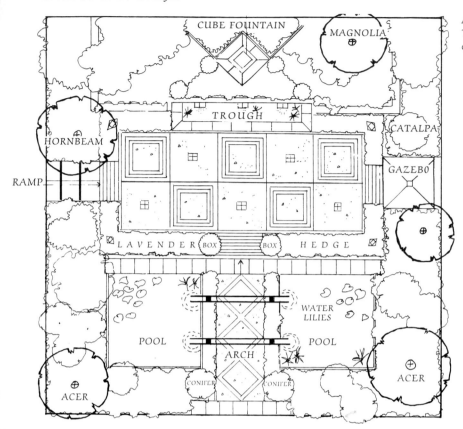

Labels within the plan: CUBE FOUNTAIN, MAGNOLIA, TROUGH, CATALPA, HORNBEAM, GAZEBO, RAMP, LAVENDER, BOX, BOX, HEDGE, POOL, WATER LILIES, POOL, ARCH, ACER, CONIFER, CONIFER, ACER

A Garden of Square Roots
This unified modern design, based on a cube theme, is tranquil and beautiful.

sage and white daisies. Mirrors set at 45° reflect the play of the water. The cube 'theme' is picked up elsewhere, with four mirror-surfaced metallic cubes symmetrically sited in each corner of the courtyard.

At floor level the grid of the squares is maintained effectively with five squares of dark grey stable pavers set in a gravel base. By turning the paving patterns through 45° along the entrance path, an effective dynamic is introduced, but within the courtyard the 90° angles are reasserted by the cuneiform shape of the gazebo. Grid-like open trellis forms the walls, and these in turn create decorative geometric patterns of light on the floor.

None of this squareness is obtrusive in any way. Detail is subtle rather than demanding, and one is not over-aware of it as a theme. Yet because of this simplicity, the balance and harmony of the garden is maintained.

THE PLANTING Beautiful planting softens the whole effect, for here again the designer has unified the design with massed planting blocks. *Cleome spinosa* and *Nicotiana sylvestris* are bold plants to be massed in this way, but they were selected to work well with the impact of the design. Backing plants like *Viburnum rhytidophyllum*, laurels, *Magnolia grandiflora* and a magnificent accent of a fastigiate hornbeam are all powerful images in their own right and frame the courtyard with their architectural presence. Nevertheless, a lot of the charm of the garden is maintained by softer detailed planting, as with surrounding low hedges of lavender adding fragrant charm, and the velvety, silver textures of *Stachys lanata* providing tactile softness elsewhere.

Aware that straight lines and right angles can be harsh, Barbara chose plants which would gently relieve this formality. Feather textures like the foliage of *Chamaecyparis pisifera* 'Aurea' with *Artemisia* 'Powis Castle' and the fluffy flowers of *Astilbe* 'Amethyst' ease the regularity of the planting pattern. More dramatic forms like *Nicotiana sylvestris* and *Cleome spinosus* have already been described as being equal to the task of balancing the dominant structures of the garden, but they are mitigated by the less ambitious, double-flowered pink *Argyranthemum* 'Vancouver', the Dutch lavender and *Alchemilla mollis*.

Movement, too, features in the selection of plants. The large yellow leaves of *Catalpa bignonioides* 'Aurea' and the very graceful, silver-backed leaves of *Acer saccharinum* 'Wieri' are never still. An unusual *Magnolia tripetala* has lusciously large, light green leaves which also stir in every breeze and, as part of the enclosing boundary, the foliage of *Phyllostachys aurea* is always restless.

A further binding link between all these chosen plants is gentle use of colour. Most of the plants are either silver grey or light lime green. As the

Below: In the evening light the garden with its recycled 'timber' arch looks inviting. In the second picture the striking forms of *Cleome spinosus* in front of the gazebo are lit by the sun. Water trickles down a chain into a pool below.

colour of all the 'timber' features is a woody grey, rather like weathered cedar, the many silvery overtones that grace the garden blend particularly well with the structures.

Flirting with this simple colour scheme are the pink flowers of the cleome and argyranthemum, with lighter mauve found in the astilbe and bluer lilac tones of the lavender. These cool pinks are echoed in the carpet planting near the fountain, where *Ajuga reptans* 'Bauherz' adds purple foliage amongst *Helichrysum* 'Limelight', canary-yellow feverfew (*Chrysanthemum parthenium*) and *Lamium maculatum* 'Aureum', which has mauve-pink flowers.

Thus, despite this being such a very rectangular and modern design, the planting is soothingly graceful and skilled, producing an overall feeling of familiarity.

RECYCLED MATERIALS I have written the word 'timber' in quotation marks, which requires explanation. One of the major features of this stylish design is that recycled materials have been used. Obviously, this is environmentally important. Neither the 'timber' nor the pergola and gazebo are real wood; they are actually made from recycled polystyrene waste, such as that which is left over from industrial production, packaging materials and food containers. It feels and looks like real timber, and is so convincing that few people realize it is a substitute. The grain of wood, its strength and longevity, are all duplicated. It can be worked as timber, that is, it can be sawn, drilled, nailed, glued and jointed. The manufacturer has produced trellis, paviours and furniture by the same means. Reassuringly, the garden combines many recycled materials most effectively. This must be the way forward to a 'greener' twenty-first century.

CASE STUDY
Timber Decking at a Lower Level

In this next garden, designed by Victor Shanley, you can see how timber works very well with brick in a modern sunken garden, as in the photograph opposite. The same timber has been used to make extremely strong retaining walls, this time stacked vertically and providing terraced levels for planting the steep sides.

THE LAYOUT This design is not symmetrical, but is formal yet comfortably spacious to use. The steps are very wide and lead up diagonally to a ground-level second garden. From here, a further flight of steps with a beautifully patterned timber balustrade, also designed by Victor, leads up to a first-floor garden which is in fact a large timber-decked roof garden above the house extension.

Wood and brick are the materials which link the whole design. Both gardens are floored with timber decking, which is as warm to look at as to walk upon. Here again, a severely geometric plan works extremely well as a vehicle for displaying magnificent lush plants.

Timber decking looks magnificent with the dark, rough texture of railway sleepers.

THE PLANTING A fine specimen of *Cordyline australis* thrives in this protected situation. Its powerfully architectural form is softened by the fresh green, pinnate foliage of *Sorbaria aitchisonii*. At the lower levels where there is little sunshine, evergreen yellow- and white-splashed forms of *Euonymus fortunei* provide colour all year round, accompanied by *Hedera helix* 'Goldheart', *Vinca minor*, *Cotoneaster dammeri* and *C. horizontalis* 'Variegatus', plus ferns. Many of the plants hang or trail over the timber walls. At a higher, sunnier level there are cluster-flowered roses, lavatera, argyranthemum, fuchsia, day lilies, lavender, santolina and recumbent blue and green conifers. The richly foliaged planting is attractive during most of the year, and builds flowery and foliaged walls worthy of Babylon but very firmly in the latter half of this century.

CASE STUDY

Contemporary Reflections upon the Past

Back to symmetry again. How often it pleases. The small garden shown in the photograph below is a design by George Carter. Clearly, presentation of the central focal summerhouse is the *raison d'être* of the garden. Approached on an axis from the gate and flanked on either side by timber obelisks, the rhythm of the garden is entirely symmetrically balanced. The work of this designer is particularly interesting, as he draws inspiration from the past while at the same time producing uniquely modern gardens. Historical formal images are interpreted with well-proportioned grace. This breaks away from the traditional garden style of lawns edged with borders of mixed planting, where there is a tendency to over-fussy colours and textures: the designer is more interested in creating sculptural forms within bounded space, elegantly alluding to mysteries.

This garden conveys a sense of theatre with its bold, elegant symmetry.

Fine laths of timber create an elegant
pergola with sculptural simplicity.

CREATING A MOOD   An air of melancholia pervades the gardens of
this designer. More than pretty assemblages of plants, they are an art
form in which space is articulated on a human scale, yet there is also a
feeling of detachment. Nature is expressively controlled. Sculpted plants
organize the spaces into intimate or grand areas. The past has a spectral
presence; blocks of clipped yew and low hedges of box hark back to
gardens which are related singularly to man, rather than those of
romanticized nature as in the sense of the 'picturesque'. But where herbs
and flowers may have floundered within the spaces, instead fantasy
elements of topiaried shapes, obelisks and balls of silver and gold are
unexplained dramatic sculptures.

This garden has a theatricality of suspended time. There is a stillness
which fosters a contemplative mood. There is nothing mundane or
sentimental. Decisive choices are made which are nevertheless
subservient to the whole charisma of the garden. The witty translation of
old garden forms into contemporary garden use is highly personal and
original, and I find the gardens have a light touch and offer themselves
invitingly as walk-in sculptures.

Using light to define form and space is the other preoccupation of this
designer. Dark, bounded entrances lead into light-filled openness. A

sense of theatre pervades, where the scene is one of an enclosed stage upon which static, sculptured plants and silvered spheres hold court. It is this feeling, combined with the allusions to times long past, which makes his work compulsively inviting. Both these themes mean that the selection of plant material must fulfil these two purposes. The three-dimensional potential of plants is utilized, just as one would model clay, for desired effect. Most are formed in a strictly geometric manner and often placed to create axial parallels or small alleys within the garden.

Another garden designed by George Carter, shown in the photograph on page 125, is on a roof. It too uses clipped plant forms and trellis; being so high, screening has a practical as well as decorative function. Decking is ideal, as it is lightweight and allows the roof below to carry the water away to gutters and pipes. Wood is cool to walk on in summer, but warm and attractive in cold weather. Here again the imagery refers back to pre-eighteenth-century European style, yet the work is entirely modern in character.

All the gardens shown in this chapter are firmly constructed in a geometric manner. They are quite different from one another, but all would work well with modern architectural ideas. They would suit newly designed concrete, glass or timber houses, or can adapt to modern apartments. The ideas are deployed simply and the planting is very carefully considered. I have to confess here to feeling an acute need for minimalism and admiring the work of Luis Barragan, but such extreme restraint is probably not suited to a temperate climate where light is cooler and plants so welcoming. There are, however, other ideas with which fertile imaginations are experimenting, as will be shown in the final chapter. Meanwhile, may I suggest that we try to create some gardens for our own time, if only to give people of the late twenty-first century something to be nostalgic about.

9 · An Alternative View

'I greatly admire the past and can be as drawn to it as anyone else, but I also feel that creativity cannot simply come to a full stop.'

Who says that there should be rules? Should any creative person submit to constraints which may inhibit their imagination? The past few chapters have been about the great differences in garden character and the aims of owners and designers. I have shown how they fulfilled these by thoughtful creativity and selection, which gradually ripened into the matured end product.

To create style in a small space you have to be clear-headed as well as creative. You need boldness. You may want to be original. You may choose to be eclectic. I hope that the previous pages have been useful in assisting the reader to sort out what is really wanted and how this can be effected.

In this chapter I am interested in how the fertile imagination is unique and ever-curious. Creative drive can be explored and expanded in a multitude of ways, and history shows us that human imagination has few limits. Narrow experience, social inertia and, sadly, all too often an empty purse, can depress the creative impulse. The development of the visual arts certainly shows an historic pattern of wavelengths, with crests and troughs. As a generation we could be in either, but we each have only our three score years and ten so we may as well try, letting the future judge whether it was worth it.

INFLUENCES AND EXPERIMENTATION

The past is, of course, the stabilizing launch pad – only neolithic cave painters could be said to be creative virgins. The rest of us acquire visual and creative stimuli from birth, and this provides the cultural framework in which we build. It is impossible to shed your culture; Westerners rarely make good Japanese gardens, and for the same reasons the traditional English garden will always reflect the luxury of huge choice when it comes to plant material.

So, keeping one's eye in, and looking at the garden designers of this century, the explorations of Lutyens, Tunnard and Jellicoe in Britain and of Farrand, Church and Halprin in the USA can be very illuminating for both garden design and landscaping. Similar rhythms of development in Europe, South America and the Far East all help to excite the imagination. In the same manner, an awareness of where the visual arts have taken us, good or bad, is an inspirational *'hors d'oeuvre'*. But I would suggest that one's own experimentations, playing with materials, both natural and man-made, can be the best way of releasing your own creativity. What do I mean?

A child at play school is unafraid of being unable to 'draw a straight line'. The messy paint experience of early days has no need of colour theory, and the picture showing Mum, partly as a head, which you love, arms which hold you, and legs which carry you around, has no need of a body, because that doesn't matter much to you at three. This enviable freedom cannot, of course, survive into adulthood. We may trail some 'clouds of glory', but mostly we adopt the adult world as it is presented to us in our own cultures. We do increase our experience, but this channels and narrows the creative process.

Nevertheless, a couple of hours every so often playing with colour yourself can be a most freeing experience. If you are very tentative, do a large scribble and fill in the shapes with different colour, then try to progress to just simple, meaningless marks of colour as you see it in front of you, without form or literal meaning. You can then place your 'work', 'mess', 'experiment', whatever you choose to call it, at a distance and you will see that some colours are far more dominant, like reds, whereas others peacefully recede, like blues. It becomes interesting, too, that colours alter their role as the light changes, and that whites and pale blues can be lustrous in a darker setting whereas pastels will fade in very strong light – the brilliance of colours used by Gauguin in the bright light of Tahiti was a direct result of the move from Brittany, where the light was cooler and bluer.

You become aware also that some colours look good together, that they can emphasize or reduce each other's effectiveness. You can see that colours affect one another, that a bright yellow next to a dark purple can be quite alarming, but a dark yellow (ochre) next to lilac can change the relationship and mood completely.

COLOUR AND MOOD

This leads on to the effect of colour on mood. It is commonly acknowledged that ladies who sing the blues are sad, that yellow is a colour of cheerfulness and friendship, and that red is the colour of drama or alarm. Furthermore, as already observed earlier, green, in all its variety, is the ever-present calm mood-maker of gardens. But other colour choices can be very influential.

'Tranquillity' is probably top of the league when it comes to feelings about gardens. In many cultures gardens have been seen as a solace, places which are calm and non-threatening. Whether they also serve religious or philosophical purposes, or just a need to raise the drawbridge against a challenging world, the garden is often described as a haven of peace and comfort. Then too, however, gaiety and cheerfulness are mentioned nearly as often. But, as stated earlier, I have no truck with 'riot'. Colourful plants can be crammed together thoughtlessly and produce nothing but a a jangled effect. I do not understand where the phrase 'riot of colour' comes into gardens. This is an angry word of protest... in a garden?

COLOUR THROUGH FOLIAGE

Sh=Shrub
H=Herbaceous
G=Grass

Green
Acer palmatum 'Little Princess' Sh
A. p. dissectum 'Viridis' Sh
A. p. 'Osakazuki' Sh
Alchemilla mollis H
Bupleurum fruticosum Sh
Choisya 'Aztec Pearl' Sh
C. ternata Sh
Ferns
Griselinia Sh
Hebe Sh
Hemerocallis H
Hosta vars H
Liriope spicata H
Pittosporum tenuifolium 'Irene Patterson' Sh
Prunus laurocerasus Sh

Grey-silver
Artemisia Sh
Brachyglottis Sh
Buddleja 'Nanho Blue' Sh
Cistus Sh
Convolvulous cneorum Sh
Cytisus battandieri Sh
Elaeagnus commutata Sh
E. augustifolia Sh
Hebe Sh
Lavandula Sh
Macleaya cordata H
Melianthus major H
Phormium tenax Sh
Romneya coulteri Sh
Rosa rubrifolia Sh
Rubus thibetanus 'Silver Fern' Sh
Salix lanata Sh
Salvia argentea H
Santolina chamaecyparisus Sh
Stachys lanata H
Verbascum broussa H

Blue
Crambe maritima H
Echinops ritro H
Festuca glauca G
Helictotrichon sempervirens G
Hosta cultivars H
Ruta graveolens Sh
Thalictrum flavum glaucum H

Red/brown
Acer palmatum vars Sh
Berberis thunbergii 'Atropurpurea' Sh
Cercis canadensis 'Forest Pansy' Sh
Cimicifuga racemosa 'Purpurea' H
Cordyline australis 'Torbay Red' Sh
Corylus maxima 'Atropurpurea' Sh
Cotinus coggygria 'Royal Purple' Sh

Euphorbia dulcis 'Chameleon' H
Foeniculum 'Giant Bronze' H
Heuchera 'Palace Purple' H
Imperata cylindrica 'Red Baron' G
Lobelia 'Dark Crusader' H
Phormium cultivars Sh
Pieris 'Forest Flame' Sh
Pittosporum tenufolium 'Tom Thumb' Sh
Rheum palmatum 'Atrosanguineum' H
Rodgersia aesculifolia H
Weigela florida 'Foliis Purpureis' Sh

Yellow

Acer japonicum 'Aureum' Sh
Arundinaria viridistrata Bamboo
Berberis thunbergii 'Aurea' Sh
Carex stricta 'Bowles' Golden' G
Choisya ternata 'Sundance' Sh
Cornus alba 'Aurea' Sh
Cortaderia selloana 'Gold Band' G
Filipendula ulmaria 'Aurea' H
Hedera helix 'Buttercup' Ivy
Hosta cultivars H
Melissa officinalis 'Aurea' H
Milium effusum 'Aureum' G
Philadelphus coronarius 'Aurea' Sh
Sambucus racemosa 'Plumosa Aurea' Sh

Variegated – white and cream

Alopecurus pratensis 'Aureo-variegatus' G
Brunnera macrophylla 'Hadspen Cream' H
Cornus alba 'Elegantissima' Sh
Cortaderia selloana 'Albo-lineata' G
Eleagnus pungens 'Limelight' Sh
Euonymus fortunei. 'Silver Queen' Sh
Glyceria maxima 'Variegata' G
Hedera vars Ivy
Hosta cultivars H
Ilex vars Sh
Iris foetidissima 'Variegata' H
I. pallida dalmatica 'Variegata' H
Pittosporum tenuifolium 'Garnettii' Sh
Rhamnus alaternus 'Argenteovariegata' Sh
Weigela florida 'Variegata' Sh

SPACE AND FORM

Space and form are mentioned frequently throughout the book. These are also the preoccupations of the architect and the sculptor. How do they learn? Just by reading, or by doing? Probably a mixture of both. Three-dimensional concepts appear to be more difficult to explore than colour, and space particularly is quite a difficult idea to grapple with. But if you have a specific plot in mind, use this as a framework for your experiments. Turn to the visual artists again to see how they do it.

The balance of mass and form is as crucial as rhythm is to music. Without rhythm, a sequence of notes becomes meaningless and melody is lost. Notes may be accurate, but unless there are gaps, pauses, fast bits and slow ones, musical recognition vanishes. In the same way, if all forms within a space are equally sized, that is, if nothing is of major importance and nothing subordinate, then the result is bland and without interest.

Considering all this, you may decide to make the space bigger than the forms, as in the famous gravel garden at Kyoto in Japan, where related groups of rocks rise like islands from a spacious 'sea' of gravel. Alternatively, you may prefer proportions where the 'action' part of the garden is a larger area that the 'passive' part – the paved area may be far larger than the area of grass and therefore more dominant. Either way it is your decision, but I would suggest that if the two main areas of a garden are of equal size then the result is usually the poorer for it. Putting it another way, a 'busy' carpet with equally 'busy' wallpaper can be anything but restful. Only one of them can star and claim attention, and if both attempt to dominate, the room becomes exhausting. It is all a question of balance. You could try this out by experimenting on a scaled plan of your garden space. Try dividing it up into large areas and small ones; look at paintings by Mondrian to see how he did this with great precision.

As regards form, it can be plainly geometric. Most of the furniture in your rooms will be rectangular in structure and your garden layout can follow suit. Alternatively, there are what I would call 'organic' forms, that is, forms that are the result of organic growth as one would see in the natural world. These are not the shapeless 'wavy lines' so often seen in gardens, but positive forms with slack curves and tight ones, where lines which are not quite straight lead into dynamic curves or into slow ones.

A sculptor like Henry Moore is worth looking at closely. His work shows a feeling for the dynamic of growth and the tension between powerful forms and softer ones. You may also find ideas from looking at photographs taken by electron microscopes, which show minute detail of the forces of growth. Further inspiration may come from examining or drawing bones, horns and antlers, shells of all types, the skeletal structure of a leaf, the crystalline structure of rocks, the kidney-shapes of haematite, patterns of the honeycomb, of feathers, of fish or branches of trees, and so forth.

If this appears whimsical or beyond you as a means of forming a design in your garden, then stick to simple geometry. It never lets you down.

Most of the gardens in this book are constructed that way. But do also remember the human appeal of the winding flow of rivers or waves on a shore, or consider the purely abstract and tactile shapes of flint, and the romantic appeal of cloud formations. A look at the amoeba shows entirely random curved form. If this inspirational world does grab you, then the sculpture of Hans Arp would prove very interesting.

TEXTURE

As well as form and colour, the word texture is often used in the garden context. The roughness of the leaf of *Viburnum rhytidophyllum* when compared with the velvet 'rabbit ears' of *Stachys lanata* are familiar contrasts. At a distance the texture seen from a window in the house is largely that of patterns; of vertical forms like yucca with horizontal ones like the flowers of lacecap hydrangeas, or of simple rounded forms like *Rodgersia tabularis* with the hazy flowers of gypsophila or some of the grasses. But as one gets closer, pattern becomes more intimate and detailed. For example, mossy saxifrages are quite different in texture from the crisply fleshy sedums, and glossy foliage, like that of *Griselinia littoralis*, reflects light, whereas the matt leaves of *Cotinus coggygria* absorb it. Contrasts such as these can create rich brocade patterns amongst plants.

Expanding your awareness of texture by making collages for fun, where anything from dried pulses to pieces of sponge or sandpaper with satin can go, is cheap and easy to experiment with and in this way your tactile sensibilities explore potential which can be put to good use in the garden. The work of Kurt Schwitters, who included old bus tickets in his collages, could open doors for you.

INSPIRATION FOR THE FUTURE

All of this may seem very pretentious, and I apologize if this is so. But extraordinary adventures have taken place in the arts, as can be seen in the architectural work of Le Corbusier, the shape of the former Goetheanum in Switzerland or indeed Gaudi's cathedral in Barcelona and Hundertwasser's apartments in Vienna. These makers opened their eyes and their minds to experiment. Finding inspiration elsewhere is open to all of us, whether it be pre-Columbian art or the classical landscape paintings of France. Such 'seeing' is never wasted.

We are now at a point in time where the calendar marks a major change. The new century approaches, and even in garden design styles will alter. We have a long way to go in the 'field' of gardens, taking them seriously as an art form as well as a wonderful horticultural display. Inspirational sources are around us if we care to look. I expect too that technology will increasingly intervene as new materials as well as plants become available. Exciting landscaping is evident in many countries and perhaps you may like to 'have a go' in your own gardens.

I have chosen three gardens here which are all personal and original. They are recently made and are expressive, witty and exploratory in different ways. Consequently some of the images are unfamiliar to many of us – but that, of course, will change with time.

CASE STUDY

A Garden for Contemplation

The first garden was designed by Lucy Gent. The site created problems with levels but, as so often happens, when these were resolved, the 'bones' of the design were formed.

As the land rises steeply from the house, one logical answer would have been to terrace it. Indeed, the area immediately beside the house was designed by an architect and is a levelled, geometrically planned terrace with steps. It is parallel with the building and consists of symmetrically sited raised beds, backed by wall and trellis, with a centrally placed opening which leads to the steeply inclined garden beyond. On either side of the entrance two pleached lime trees reinforce the symmetry, whilst also marking the division of space within the garden area as a whole.

THE LAYOUT Upon this set, the designer tackled the natural topography in an intuitive and original way. One enters a space with few straight lines and sensuous, unravelling curves. To one side a 30cm (12in) wide mowing strip encloses a curved planting bed, which sweeps down from the far corner gate. This sinuous line passes by an enclosed seating area, and culminates in a perfect spiral, within which is a nucleus of three currant bushes, red, white and black. At its heart is a saucer-shallow ceramic bird bath by Sarah Walton.

The plan clearly shows the sinuous line of muted yellow brick paving, as it describes a full curve from the spiral and up around a wide planting bed to the gate at the top left-hand corner. Taking advantage of an existing opening, the dynamic curve of the planting bed flows through to a hidden garden beyond the gate. These sweeping lines are all centred geometric parts of circles, which makes them pleasingly full. However, because the land rises so steeply, the curves look more abstract than geometric and this adds a gently mystic feel to the garden. It is interesting to remember how the classic orders of ancient Greek architecture applied deception to create mathematical order; that is, the columns were slightly curved in profile so that the brightness of light did not impinge upon the shaft, which would have made them look thinner and insubstantial. In this garden the reverse is true. Mathematical precision has been distorted by the slope of the site, creating an illusion of abstract form.

Up in the top right-hand corner of the garden, timber and gravel steps climb, with mildly twisting form, to a shaded platform beneath three silver birches. From here the view back is of dips and curves and nothing is static. The steps are inviting to ascend and also to look at, and they are wide enough for a series of plant containers to be placed at intervals.

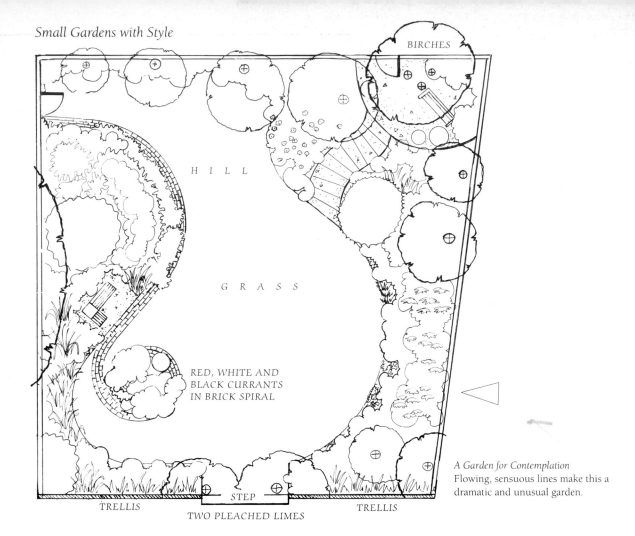

BIRCHES

HILL

GRASS

RED, WHITE AND
BLACK CURRANTS
IN BRICK SPIRAL

STEP

TRELLIS

TWO PLEACHED LIMES

TRELLIS

A Garden for Contemplation
Flowing, sensuous lines make this a
dramatic and unusual garden.

If I have a criticism it is that people are left with a rather steep grassy
slope to negotiate on the left of the garden – the mowing strip is not
really a substitute for a path. This could be overcome by making entirely
functional and easily concealed steps behind the large border, which
would please the owners and satisfy the designer's wish to present an
unmarked lawn.

THE PLANTING The planting pattern observes the same feeling of
movement. Following the brick edging, an inner curve winding down the
hill is marked out by a loose hedge of *Aster laterifolius*. This brilliant plant
grows to 45cm (18in) and becomes a mass of light pinkish blue flowers
in late autumn. The curve divides the bed, separating larger shrubs and
small trees, including *Catalpa bignonoides* 'Aurea' and a multi-stemmed
strawberry tree (*Arbutus unedo*), from lower herbaceous plants in front.

Reaffirming the serpentine rhythm by planting Australian fountain
grass (*Penisetum alepecuriodes*) along the fullest part of the curve, Lucy
runs the planting pattern down to another Australian plant, this time the
silvered *Astelia nervosa*. Though no taller than 60cm (2ft), the leaves are
light, reflecting silvered swords. It catches the light, and the eye, from

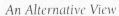

Left: A seat is flanked by silvered *Astelia nervosa* and *Phormium cookianum variegatum.*

Above: The brick spiral wraps itself around three currant bushes.

Below: Revelling in the natural curves of the topography, the designer has created sweeps of form in the planting beds and the gently twisting steps.

Geranium wallichianum 'Buxton's Blue'
entwines beautifully with *Clematis texensis*.

everywhere in the garden, and marks a transition between the dynamic
sweep of the border and the static paved rectangle that provides another
place to sit, this time in the sunlight. Within this and all the other
planting beds, the designer has continually linked the planting patterns.
Artemisias flow into euphorbias, golden lamium into stachys, anthemis
into golden marjoram, and all are bound together, almost literally, by a
rambling blue *Clematis durandii*.

In other areas of the garden, planting is carried out with the same
spirited continuity. As the seasons change, plants merge into one another
and colour relationships subtly alter. From hellebores to hydrangeas, the
changes of colour and texture are gentle and pleasing. Nothing jars, as all
the plants are chosen with visual as well as horticultural compatibility in
mind. It is noticeable in this garden how rare plants, like the 'kowhai' of
New Zealand (*Sophora tetraptera*), mingle with those of more modest
birth, namely herbs like comfrey, feverfew and alliums – this garden is
plant-sensitive rather than horticulturally grand. More clematis, in this
case *C. texensis*, ingratiates itself over a prostrate ceanothus and *Senecio
leucostachys*, and along with this the small blue *Geranium wallichianum*
Buxton's Blue offers bright blue-eyed charm into late autumn as it
perambulates amongst its greater peers. *Artemisias* like 'Powis Castle' and
A. ludoviciana 'Silver Queen' with a very attractive *Crocosmia* 'Solfatare'
work closely together, and these associations are gently referred to in one
plant, *Phlomis fruticosa*, with its grey foliage and muted yellow flowers.

It is the spirit of this garden with its unabashed sensuous forms,
intimately enfolding the topography, which makes it a highly personal
design. The garden is unusual in that it works sculpturally with the land
form instead of attacking the levels problem with a more conventional
answer, that of terracing. Carving out shapes from existing topographical
forms is working *with* nature rather than over-controlling it. It must be
noted here that the owner has been very involved with the garden from
the start. It is under her sensitive supervision and care, and she is ably
assisted by an equally committed gardener. Successful gardens are often
the result of such admirable co-operation.

CASE STUDY
A Light Touch

The next garden is far smaller, and one in which the surprise of the unpredictable makes for originality and verve. This is a backyard, wonderfully converted by Anthony Noel. Being very overlooked and fundamentally one of many clones, it must have been most unappetising before Anthony took hold of it, but he has flair and vision and has tackled the area with creative imagination. The result is a fascinating, whimsical small-space garden which changes delightfully throughout the seasons.

DESIGNING FOR SURPRISES A very tiny green-sward lawn is decoratively edged by emphasizing the randomly placed, rectangular York paving. This looks as if it is maintained by nail scissors, producing a fine, velvet texture of moss. At one side of the garden a black garden chair becomes a throne, flanked by dignitaries of red phormium on either side, but alleviated by floating drapes of *Lathyrus latifolius albiflorus*. Across from this, a small wall fountain bubbles into a water trough, on which are displayed old watering cans recycled and striped in Wedgwood green and white.

Witty topiary mixes clipped balls of box with identically-sized stone ball finials placed soldierly along the wall, as seen in the photograph on page 136. Oversized containers, reminiscent of Jellicoe's large, surreal Roman urns at Sutton Place, are as startling and powerful as they are

Two red phormiums flank the 'throne' of a black single-seater iron chair, while curtains of white *Lathyrus latifolius* drape themselves behind.

Above: Witty juxtaposition of clipped topiary balls alongside identical stone finials on the wall opposite the black 'throne' raise a smile.

Right: The beauty of lilies and daturas distract all eyes from the office block beyond the garden. Hostas, petunias and marguerites add pastel shades and more white. Ivy-clad walls act as backing and scented foliage abounds.

unexpected. The designer's lighthearted approach to garden design has created this innovative and charming plot in which there are continual surprises.

Anthony has a marvellous eye for colour and humour, as can be seen in the decorative painting of mundane objects, like the old watering cans already referred to. His choice of 'ice cream' colours, pistachio and pale strawberry, create a happy sense of summer. Entirely in character, the flower colours come out in sympathy. Tiny pink-striped roses, in painted pots, nodding pink-striped *Clematis* 'Étoile Rose' and the darkly richer tones of *C.* 'Royal Velours' with *C.* 'Etoile Violette' are echoed extremely effectively in other parts of the garden.

And yet there are strong forms, there are exotics, there are surprises. Clipped forms create anchors; rigid agave in urns provide sculpture; a datura adds exotic fragrance and drama. Everywhere there is an unpredictable juxtaposition of plants, of static forms alongside fabulous flummery. The designer does not regard gardens as so sacred that one must not err. Playing around with ideas and alternating some every year, makes this a garden of delightful changes. He is not overawed by the correctness of scale or plant association but, with confident sensitivity and wit, pleases himself. That others are charmed as well is a bonus.

And behind all this is a large ungracious red-brick office block – but who has time to notice?

CASE STUDY
The Prêt à Porter Garden

And now for something completely different. The notion of transplanting a garden has occurred in the past: it is horticulturally possible to dig up mature trees, lavish love upon them and transplant them into a new home. But Paul Cooper, an innovative sculptor turned garden designer, takes this much further – and the whole garden may be packed up and taken away. As he says, many people live in rented accommodation, but should they deny themselves a garden? Very few people are prepared to spend money on a conventional garden, if all that is likely to happen is that their efforts prove to be an investment for their landlord.

This garden is a packable and transportable steel-framed structure which can be easily assembled on site. You bring it with you in the

Again the humour of the designer raises a smile. This David Hockney-inspired mural is far removed from the *trompe l'oeil* paintings of the past. Steel trees will never shed their foliage, while decking is warm underfoot.

removal van. It can be connected with water and light sources and provides a planting scheme, sitting area and even a water-course.

As well as steel, the construction uses timber. The first provides the framework, pergola, seating and sculptured trees – 'for winter'. The second provides flooring as a welcoming contrast. The garden employs many new materials, including a semi-opaque windbreak wall that does away with the 'shady border' but creates an excellent environment for both plants and people. Furnishings include weatherproof fabric bean bags, great for children or adults, and for the plants, over-the-shoulder 'growbags'. This is a garden that can be built virtually anywhere – on a roof, in a concrete yard, and anywhere with difficult access. In fact, this garden can boldly go where no garden has gone before.

All the plants are in containers and can be altered to suit circumstances and seasons. Some, however, are permanent. Three trees rise above you with steel mesh 'palm' leaves. These sculptured plants are the reliable 'evergreens', wittily alluding to the need for permanent 'all-year-round' planting. Timber decking and a swing seat add a welcoming and 'homely' touch. Around the perimeter is a canal-like water garden which holds dwarf water lilies. It is covered by slim metal grating through which the lilies can be appreciated and on top of which you may safely tread. At the far end, with a hint of Hockney, a mural provides an amusing background which is light years away from the *trompe-l'oeil* paintings of the past. Paul adds, with satisfaction, that all the elements are moveable so you can rearrange them at will; in other words, the owner's participation is invited, so creative possibilities are extended.

There have always been originals; different thinkers with their own ideas. Sometimes they initiate change and sometimes not. It doesn't really matter, so long as we always make room for them. But owners as well as designers have some responsibility here. Designs cost money, and I fully understand that this can inhibit those who are to spend it. Liking to 'know what you are getting' beforehand, and being sure that it conforms to a standard, is the way that many of us make our purchases. But if this were always so, the whole world would be a reproduction of the past, a pastiche of other styles. Surely we esteem ourselves sufficiently to go sometimes into uncharted waters? I am a garden lover, I greatly admire the past and can be as drawn to it as anyone else, but I also feel that creativity cannot simply come to a full stop. So garden owners – who are the patrons just as in Rennaisance Italy – and the media could encourage new ideas and, better still, explore some themselves.

Bibliography

Archer-Wills, Anthony. *The Water Gardener* (Frances Lincoln, 1993)

Beales, Peter. *Classic Roses* (Collins Harvill, 1986)

Billington, Jill. *Architectural Foliage* (Ward Lock, 1991)

Bloom, Alan. *Moisture Gardening* (Faber & Faber, 1966)

Boisset, Caroline, (ed). *The Garden Sourcebook* (Mitchell Beazley, 1993)

—— *The Plant Growth Planner* (Mitchell Beazley, 1992)

Brookes, John. *John Brookes' Garden Design Book* (Dorling Kindersley, 1991)

Chatto, Beth. *The Damp Garden* (Dent, 1983)

—— *The Dry Garden* (Dent, 1983)

Church, Thomas. *Gardens are for People* (McGraw Hill, 1983)

Cox, Jeff. *Creating a Garden for the Senses* (Abbeville Press, 1993)

Dodson, Harry. *Harry Dodson's Practical Kitchen Garden* (BBC, 1992)

Ferguson, Nichola. *Right Plant, Right Place* (Pan, 1984)

Gray-Wilson, Christopher and Mathews, V. *Gardening on Walls* (Collins, 1983)

Hardy Plant Society. *The Plant Finder* (Headmain Ltd, 1993/4)

Heritage, Bill. *Ponds and Water Gardens* (Blandford, revised 1990)

Hobhouse, Penelope. *Colour in Your Garden* (Collins, 1985, and Boston Little Brown, 1985)

Huxley, Anthony. *The Penguin Encyclopaedia of Gardening* (Penguin, 1981)

Jackson, Sheila. *Blooming Small: A City Dweller's Garden* (Herbert Press, 1993)

Joyce, David. *Pruning and Training Plants* (Mitchell Beazley, 1992)

King, Ronald. *The Quest for Paradise* (Mayflower Books, 1979)

Lacey, Stephen. *Scent in Your Garden* (Frances Lincoln, 1991)

Larkcom, Joy. *Oriental Vegetables* (John Murray, 1991)

Lauderdale, Wendy. *The Garden at Ash Tree Cottage* (Weidenfield & Nicolson, 1993)

Lloyd, Christopher. *Foliage Plants* (Collins, 1985)

—— *The Well-tempered Garden* (Collins, 1985)

Lyall, Sutherland. *Designing the New Landscape* (Thames & Hudson, 1991)

Page, Russell. *The Education of a Gardener* (Collins, 1983)

Paul, Anthony and Rees, Yvonne. *The Water Garden* (Windward/Frances Lincoln, 1988)

Phillips, Roger and Rix, Martin. *Perennials* Vols I and II (Pan, 1993)

Reader's Digest Encyclopaedia of Garden Plants (1984)

Reader's Digest Guide to Creative Gardening (1984)

Rose, Graham. *The Low Maintenance Garden* (Windward, 1983)

Royal Horticultural Society Concise Encyclopaedia of Gardening Techniques (Mitchell Beazley, 1981)

Scott-James, Ann. *Perfect Plants, Perfect Gardens* (Summit Books, 1988)

Stevens, David. *Town Gardens* (Conran Octopus, 1992)

Stuart-Thomas, Graham. *The Art of Planting* (Dent, 1984)

—— *Ornamental Shrubs, Climbers and Bamboos* (John Murray, 1992)

—— *Perennial Garden Plants* (Dent/RHS, 1982)

Tunnard, Christopher. *Gardens in the Modern Landscape* (Architectural Press, 1938)

Acknowledgements

Firstly I have to thank Bill, my husband, for his constant support and encouragement ever since we met. I would also like to thank Lucy Gent for her interest and considerable help throughout.

I was fortunate to work on this book with the photographer Clive Nichols whose professionalism and patience produced most of the excellent photographs, and I am very grateful to Marianne Majerus for further beautiful photographs (pages 45, 49, 64, 68–9, 81, 124) and Ian Pleeth for the photograph on pages 116–17. All other photographs were taken by the author.

Thanks are also due to those clients of mine who sustained us with coffee, bagels and oatcakes on early morning 'shoots'. They are: John and Karin Welz (Chapter 1), Lorna McKeand (Chapter 1), Sharon and Alan Beuthin (Chapter 2), Max McGuire and Nicholas Drake (Chapter 2), Margaret Yates (Chapter 4), Gilly Gallagher (Chapter 4), Beverly and Sidney Austin (Chapter 7), Rob and Kay Kinnear (Chapter 7).

I have also benefited greatly from the friendship and generosity of designer colleagues whose work is shown in this book: Elizabeth Whateley (Chapter 2), Victor Shanley (Chapter 4, 7, 8), Lucy Gent (Chapters 6 and 9), Barbara Hunt (Chapter 8), George Carter (Chapter 8), Anthony Noel (Chapter 9), and Paul Cooper (Chapter 9). The author designed gardens in Chapters 1, 2, 4, 7, and 8.

I must also thank garden owners for welcoming us and sharing their gardens. They are Lorna McKeand (Chapter 1), Wendy Lauderdale (Chapter 3), Mr and Mrs Rupert de Zoate (Chapter 5), Dr and Mrs Peter Taylor (Chapter 5), Peter Partridge (Chapter 6), Myles Challis (Chapter 6), Sheila Jackson (Chapter 6), Sir Anthony and Lady Bamford (Chapter 7), Mr Press (Chapter 8) and Pat Kavanagh (Chapter 9)

Finally, thanks is due especially to Linda Tyler who coped with layers of manuscripts and red ink with fortitude and skill.

Index